CHAPTER O

May 29th, 2004

It was a beautiful sunny morning in the Saudi Arabian Peninsula ....

I had a few more minutes today before the bus came to take me to the Oasis compound where I worked as a nursery assistant. I loved my job it took me away from my life on the compound and gave me a purpose each morning. It was a taste of the real world. Women were not allowed to work in Saudi Arabia, a few jobs that were available were mainly in the teaching and nursing areas .These vacancies were very few and far between and not advertised freely. Every day I worked at the school it was so rewarding to watch the children develop and gain new skills. Whatever race, creed and colour a child is they are all the same worldwide, they have the same passion to learn and play.

My husband David gave me a kiss as I left the villa. I headed towards the bus stop, a bit slower today, I was four and half months pregnant with my little boy Jacob. We were so excited to meet him in a few months time. At thirty six being pregnant was a lot more tiring than with my previous pregnancies. My Daughter Aimee was now eighteen, and my son Ben was fifteen almost adult. I reached the entrance to the compound and said good morning to the security guards in the gatehouse, I stepped outside to wait for my bus to arrive . I did feel especially good today, David had bought me a new Maternity dress it was more comfortable for working at the school, not a lot of my clothes fitted me due to my developing baby bump. I looked heavily pregnant for four and a half months, I could of easily of passed as nearly full term! I was beginning to wonder if there was more than one baby in there!

Aimee, my daughter had called me about three days after I had found out I was pregnant with the exciting news that she too was expecting a baby, I didn't know what to say as it felt so strange that my daughter and I were pregnant together. My friends and family thought it was quite amusing that David and I would become grandparents, and of course over the moon to have two babies arriving so close together. I don't think Aimee was too impressed though as it probably didn't look right to be pregnant the same time as her mum. It was exciting all the same. The bus was on time today thankfully, the heat was starting to get to me , I knew once on the bus the air-conditioning would kick in and be comforting. The doors of the minibus opened. "Good morning Dawn" all the ladies shouted, "Good morning" I replied and found myself a seat. We headed out towards the traffic lights , we had to do a u-turn so we would be on the correct course travelling towards the Oasis compound. All the ladies were chatting and laughing as normal about their holidays coming up and what activities they had prepared for the children for the week ahead. As we approached the turning I noticed it was unusually quiet on the road today. Both sides of the road had tall buildings, offices and exits leading to the residential compounds. The Oasis compound was one of the largest well known compounds in Saudi Arabia for its extravagant furnishings and buildings. The Oasis Compound was one of the largest compounds in the Province, and consisted of Hotels, Villas, Restaurants, a Recreation Centre, Shops, a Skating Rink, a Sports Hall Gymnasiums and even had its very own Indoor Swimming Pool. Everything to meet your needs could be found here, it was exactly like its name an Oasis a place of luxurious delights, everything from the food to the décor of the hotel, everything was at its finest. It was always very decorative during the holy month of Ramadan. The rooms were adorned with beautiful Arabian Trinkets, Sheesah Pipes, it gave you the illusion that you were sitting inside a real Bedouin tent. The restaurants had many dishes and buffets on offer from all over the world Italian , Asian and Japanese etc. A lot of the staff would usually be invited for Ramadan and to special events, the food was always so spectacular and delicious.

As we travelled and turned past the first set of buildings we heard a loud cracking and piercing noise coming from outside of the bus. At first I thought one of the tyres of the bus had just blown! But the noise started to get louder and louder. What could it be? Curious a few of the ladies pulled the curtain back by the side of the window to have a look at what all the commotion was about. In the Middle East this was a typical way for ladies to travel discreetly, most of the buses had blinds or curtains to hide the faces of the females inside . Julie who was the Learning

Centre Secretary at the time said that we were not to worry and that it was just a few fire crackers going off. Feeling a little reassured and unaware what was really happening outside we carried on with our journey.

Erica and I were situated near the front of the bus next to each other where we both had a good view directly onto the front of the road. Erica was a lovely friend and always had something to laugh about, she was a pleasure to be with.

We both looked forward and could not believe our eyes! All we could see was a small pick-up truck , it had pulled up in front of the bus. A man of eastern appearance pulled his window down, he had a bandaged scarf tied around his head , he climbed out and sat on the window ledge of the truck and pulled out a very large gun . The man turned and started firing towards the security guards on the left side of the road which was the backend of the Oasis compound. I turned to Erica and we just looked at each other in disbelief. "Oh no Erica that man has a gun!" I shouted. By now the firing had got worse and we could see the return blue flashes of crossfire coming from the soldiers guns who were guarding the compound. Erica started to shout, "They have guns they have guns, whats happening why?". By now the sound of the firing was like air splitting , a loud cracking sound radiated all around us . It was so surreal could we be witnessing this really? Bewildered and confused by all of this I started to feel insecure and very frightened, I called to the bus driver, "Can you please turn around driver, can you take us back to our compound?". "No mam" the driver replied, "I think we will be safer if we carry on to the Oasis compound we will be safe there". The terrorists disappeared out of sight thankfully. Was he right ? Would we be safer inside the Oasis Compound? We were unaware of the numerous attacks going on around the Province. There had been several attacks, the first attack that had happened that morning had started at 6.45am where four terrorists had arrived at the Al Khobar Petroleum Centre where guards and employees were shot at. One American and two Filipinos were killed. One British worker Michael Hamilton had just arrived at the Apicorp Compound at 7.15am and was instantly fired upon , he was dragged from his car and then tied to another car and was dragged along the highway. He was hardly recognisable when later found, so inhumane, so tragic. An Egyptian boy had also been shot dead, he was shot whilst leaving the compound on a school bus, a poor innocent child caught up in this war of terror.

I didn't like being in this situation, already I had a sense to get off the bus and go back to the Las Dunas Compound where I lived . I knew I would at least have my family around me and be safe. By now our Driver looked very nervous and unsure if he was doing the right thing by carrying on. All the ladies on the bus turned to each other shocked and lost for words on what we had all just witnessed. I started thinking about David and Ben , had he left for work yet? Had he also heard the gunfire what was he thinking? Was he safe? What else is going on in the Province? It was no time and we had arrived at the gates of the Oasis Compound. From a short distance away I could hear more firing, it was starting to get closer and closer!....Oh no!! We are being fired at! The terrorists had more than one truck and it had been some sort of signal to the other terrorists that they could access and enter through the side of the Compound . The security guards who were protecting the gates of the compound had by now either been shot dead or had tried to run for their lives. "Mam get down.....get down! The driver shouted , at this moment I was very surprised that he hadn't been shot as was in full range of the firing, he was very brave risking his own life for all us! I lay down on the floor and looked around at my friends and thought this is the place we were all going to die here on this bus, I just waited for when.......If its going to happen please let it be quick I thought to myself. The sirens were getting louder and louder from the entrance gates to the compound. The guards by now had fled for their lives some had been shot dead. This must have been carefully planned by the terrorists as they knew the gates would be open on the arrival of our bus . Later I had learned that the terrorists had gained access through the underground skating rink and had entered through the car park underneath .

The gunmen took their positions on the rooftops of the villas we were surrounded, they started searching villa by villa slaying people who were not Muslims and burning the residents out of their homes . All the ladies on the bus by now were lying face down on the floor, we shielded ourselves from stray bullets that could possibly come

through the buses framework at any second
.

I reached for my phone and called David.

David's phone started to ring , 8:03 one of those visual moments that remain in your memory, 8:03 clear as day on my watch every time I recall that day, Saturday 29th May, 2004; 8:03.

David was sitting in work talking to his friend and work colleague when his mobile had rung, "Hi Dawn how are you my love?" David could hear the fear the panic in my voice ..."Where are you?" Still the distant crack of rapid gunfire was all around us.

I had to be firm and strong and replied , "Please listen we are being shot at I don't think I am going to make it , I am lying on the floor of the bus they are shooting from behind us at the guards its so very near, we are on the compound the driver said we would be safe here."

"Yes that`s the best place to be," David and I were unaware that the terrorists were already inside the compound.
"Dawn I can hear the sound of the compound siren in the background now".
"Dawn , I am coming to get you". I know he would try and get to me but he wouldn't be allowed anywhere near the compound.

"Dave I love you, I may not see you again."

"I love you too Dawn, you will be alright, the drivers right, the best place to be is on the compound, I will come and get you". "David I am going now, oh please tell the children I will always love them, I am so sorry..... Goodbye."

"You will be okay Dawn, I will call you when I get there, I love you, bye"

It was a quick phone call as I knew I didn't have much time as I would either probably be shot very soon or would have to try and escape and get off the bus to safety, but where ? I am not ready to die , this wasn't and isn't my time ,how did I get caught up in all this? All these thoughts were going through my mind. This was the worst thing I had ever had to do in my life, I had to to tell my darling husband I might die and he might never see his unborn child, why did I have to do this? What gave the terrorists the right to put my family my loved ones and my friends, through this? All I could think of right now was my children without a mother, my husband without a wife, my parents , my sister ...... if its going to happen please let it be over instantly, I drifted off into my deepest conscious I could see my son and daughter playing together when they were small, I held that moment for a few minutes.

David turned to Martyn his supervisor, "It's Al-Qaeda, they are attacking the Oasis Compound, Dawn is being shot at on the bus, I am going to try and get to her, if not I will head back to Las Dunas."

"Ok no probs David you go you have to try " Martin replied.

Thoughts started to play around in my head as I drove towards Oasis, as long as Dawn gets off the bus and onto the compound everything will be fine, she and our unborn baby will be safe then the terrorists will drive somewhere else and eventually be killed or captured by the police……

I set off from work and pulled off the highway up to the lights at the Toyota Garage , as I stopped for the red light a red-crescent ambulance with flashing lights pulled up to the police car always parked at this junction. It appeared as though he was asking directions to the Oasis Compound, the policeman looked surprised as though he was unaware of what was happening but pointed in the direction of the compound. As I got within 500 metres of Oasis it became clear that I would not be able to get anywhere near to the compound there was a mass of police cars and ambulances, the only vehicles being allowed towards the Oasis Compound. I decided to turn off reluctantly and headed towards our compound, Las Dunas. The guards at both the first and second gate were unaware of what was going on but had heard gunfire and heard the sirens of the emergency vehicles ,yet they were carrying on their duties as normal, why hadn't they followed the lockdown procedure, (only allowing residents onto the compound and not allowing anyone to leave). I pulled in by the guardroom and warned the barrier/gate operators of what was going on before calling my company's security liaison representative.

"Hello Dave?"

"Hi Ivor, do you know what is happening with the attack on Oasis and are we going to lockdown?"

"Yes we will most probably very soon, both the airbase and all the compounds. I am in a meeting right now we are discussing whether we are going to lockdown, I don't know if you are aware but there are several incidences going on in the area."

"Well Oasis is under attack and we should go to lockdown, I will tell them here at Las Dunas to go to lockdown and the other compounds need to be told. I just need conformation from you. The guards here were not aware of anything going on when I arrived a few minutes ago."

"Hold on one minute Dave please", Ivor replied, "Yes David go to lockdown and we will let the other compounds know.

I hung up and instructed the guardroom to go to lockdown notifying the residents with the compound siren, and telling them if they had any issues or problems to call me. There had in the past been a few false alarms some of the compound residents would be unsure if this was a false alarm or a practice procedure. I made a few phone calls to some of the residents and asked them to pass the information on and that the Alarm was for real and to follow all procedures for lockdown. I headed my way back to the villa thinking about Dawn every minute, I felt sickened I couldn't reach her.

Meanwhile on the compound..... the machine gunfire was shooting through the air above the bus, I was so scared so frightened ...... and so alone.... I pinched my eyes together just waiting for it to be all over with. Please can I wake up now , this was all just a bad dream .....

It was so quiet here on the bus, you could smell the fear in the air of the unknown. "Mam get off the bus now Mam quick," I didn't have time to think and I listened to what the driver was telling me. I moved anxiously towards the front of the bus not knowing what was ahead of me. A few of my friends before had got off the bus but I couldn't see which way they had gone. My legs didn't want to move forward , I closed my eyes and found an inner strength to move on, I ran towards the Learning Centre it seemed the right the safest place to be right now. I reached the front door of the building , "Jo ... Jo" I bellowed as I ran through the doors of the school, " There's gunmen on the compound, Jo where are you!" Jo Was the schools learning director and a very good friend of mine. I just had to warn her , she might not know what is happening and be caught unaware. I couldn't find her anywhere suddenly I heard fast footsteps running towards the school. I quickly hid behind the door not knowing who to expect, "Dawn quick darling Pauline shouted, everyone is over the reception area quick come with me Jo is with us also". "How did you know I was here Pauline?" I asked, " We realized when we entered the reception that you were missing and my intuition was that you had come here Dawn" . As we left the school I felt so glad that the children hadn't turned up for school today, it would of been very hard hiding children and expecting them to be quiet in a situation like this, they must have been told or had heard the firing in a way they had been fortunate to have been prewarned early as a few minutes more they would have been on lockdown inside the compound with us . We were on the move again, we hurried out of the doors and outside to the open road and quickly made our way towards the doors of the reception area. Every morning you would be greeted by three men on reception who always had a smile on their faces, once a week we would take the children downstairs to the sports hall for their weekly exercise to the gymnasium . Inside the building everything was still looking as normal as it always did, from the chandeliers to the heavy marbled tables with the exquisite ornaments, what extravagance! Could this be really happening ?

Pauline helped me down the marbled steps , "Dawn are you ok, don't have the baby right now will you" she joked, "I will try not to" I replied. My stomach was sickened I was shaking and quivering so much I wasn't so sure, I started to fear the worst. When we got down to the bowling area, all of my colleagues were sitting down drinking coffee it probably hadn't really sunk in with them yet the situation we were in right now. There was an eerie feel to the room, I walked around for a minute trying to catch my breath and thought about what we should do next.

My phone started to ring...

David was calling me from his mobile, "Hi love, are you in the compound somewhere safe now?"

"We are downstairs, in the cafe having a coffee David, but I think we should all find somewhere safe to take cover , I ran off the bus, I was frightened, the driver said you must leave the bus, everybody came down here, I ran into the nursery to find Jo but she wasn't there."

" Dawn You will be alright, try and calm down and take deep breaths, I tried to get to Oasis, but it was all blocked off, I am back at Las Dunas now, we have gone to lockdown here. I am so sorry I couldn't come and rescue you, you are my world to me darling you know I would of if it were possible" (I could hear the panic in David's voice.. "Oh David please be strong" I silently spoke to myself. We said goodbye once again it was so very hard .

Once again David felt helpless and was glad of the chance to speak to me unsure if I had already been shot or injured.

David put his head in his hands and wept. He thought to himself..

I was full of confident words for Dawn, but inside I just yearned to be with her and our unborn child, to protect her as this was my duty and responsibility to her as her Husband. Helpless inside all I could do was reassure her that everything would work out right, even though I had no way of telling what would happen I needed to remain strong and positive..... "Oh god please don't hurt my precious ones please" . I wasn't a religious type of person but today if there was any truth of a higher being then I was hanging on the hope that a greater force could help us through this day.

David had instructed the guards to go to lockdown earlier, this procedure was practiced on a regular basis in case in the event of a terrorist attack this was for real. David headed his way back to the villa some of the residents were unsure and had thought as expected it that it may have been a false alarm. A couple of residents were outside their doors wondering what was going on. David advised them to go back indoors as there had been a lot of firing going on in the distance and it was best to be out of site. David had been appointed the compound security representative only just a few months ago, and had never dreamed he would actually have to put it in action and so soon. David was a good reliable man and would do his upmost to protect the residents .

My instinct now was to look for somewhere to hide! To be honest none of us knew what to do next. Jo came running into the room and shouted , "can I have some help please! The Chef has been shot in the kitchen I need a nurse now"! Luckily most of my friends were qualified nurses, Kathy replied, "I am coming straight away where is he is it bad?". I had got to know Kathy really well over the past couple of months. She was a true kind friend a breath of fresh air to the nursery, so refreshing with a heart of gold and we just connected instantly. I hope she will be alright how does she know that the terrorists that shot the chef had gone and won't come back? I didn't want Kathy to go I was afraid she would also get hurt .

The injured man's Indian friends were crying and pleading for someone to help their friend I would of done the same myself. Kathy was so brave. In no time Kathy had returned and was shocked by what she had seen, he had been shot through the cheek and partly to his brain. Kathy had bandaged him up the best she could and hurried back to us. We felt we were waiting for some time bomb to go off, not knowing what would happen next, the terrorists could attack us at any minute! It now seemed more of a reality that we could also could get hurt. Why weren't we hiding?

"Please! Please! Come with me," A small Indian man was standing in the entrance of the bowling area, "Quickly we must hide please". I was so glad so relieved ! The Indian man was walking with a laidback manner, my instinct was to hurry! Come on, come on I thought, instinct was kicking in fast. With every hurried step I took I could not stop shaking , where would we hide? I called David on my mobile phone, I hadn't spoken with him since I was in the bowling alley, for all David knew I could have been hurt or killed, every precious second counted that we could stay in contact with each other, it could be the last time… "Dawn are you okay?" David asked , "Yes I am okay thank you, I haven't been hurt but there are gunmen everywhere and we must hide now so I am now turning my phone off incase it alerts the terrorists where we are." "We are going into hiding that's all I can say we are looking for somewhere possibly safe but we don't know do we"….. "Bye David I am going to get out of here I promise you, I love you so much darling, bye" I didn't wait to hear David's reply as it would of upset me too much our time was precious we had to keep moving.

Chapter 2

had turned her phone off, I wanted to keep talking to help my wife and unborn child, yet to call would be foolish a sense of despair, I fought the despair knowing I had to remain strong as this is the only way we would get through the next few hours and defeat the mindless terrorists the thugs psychologically the next few hours would prove to be the hardest. I decided to go outside and check on some of the residents . If I kept myself busy the time would go quicker I just had to keep busy.

As I passed two neighbouring villas the two residents Jan and Paola were standing outside. I told them to go into their villas as there were a lot of terrorist incidences happening in the area and the Oasis Compound was currently under attack. Jan looked shocked, "was it actually real this time"? Jan asked, "Yes its not a false alarm Jan its real, Dawn is trapped inside the Oasis compound with all the other ladies they didn't have any warning I feel so bad I can't go and collect her", "Oh David words cannot express how you must be feeling right now, she is a good friend to us too" , Paola and Jan replied .

"Did Dawn and the other ladies manage to find somewhere to hide ?" asked Paola.

"They are on the compound hopefully in hiding somewhere safe, the last time I talked to Dawn she was hoping to find a secure place to hide, none of us are allowed to leave this compound now , no-one can re-enter either we are on lockdown". "Do you want to come in for a Coffee?" Paola asked , "You can't sit in your villa by yourself David?"

On latter reflection the invitation for a coffee seemed somewhat contradictory to the situation presenting itself around us, though it was meant in the honest and caring way as said , Paola was such a comfort right now , it showed the caring spirit of people that would present itself on many more occasions as the day progressed. Despite requesting that Jan join us, she was reluctant and preferred to be alone in her villa. Again a trait of human nature, that appears for some people at times of fear. Different people react differently in such situations and beforehand it's difficult to judge how a particular character will react in such situations.

Not long after joining Paola for a coffee, her daughter, Francesca rang from the Dhahran International British Grammar School asking what was going on, and that they had heard there was shootings happening in the Khobar area, but the teachers where not letting on. Probably not to frighten the children, but this had just fed their curiosity, and although they were not supposed to use their phones in class they had collectively decided to ignore the teachers this particular day. I asked Paola to ask her daughter to tell Ben, who was in the same class that his Mum was safe on the Oasis Compound and that I would call him after. Of course this was conjecture on my part as in reality I had no knowledge of whether Dawn and our unborn child were alive or dead, or if they were okay, and what feeling of sheer hell they must be enduring. Against my need to be there for them at all costs, even this natural responsibility I was prevented from carrying out. How selfish I was to feel so helpless when Dawn and our unborn child were experiencing the ultimate feeling of helplessness. The next few hours would be my darkest time. I was concerned for my son Ben I didn't want him to be alone and have this heavy worry on his mind, I just wanted our family to be together not all over the place, this was a normal reaction for any parent faced with this situation.

As the British news had now picked up on the events developing in the Al-Khobar, Saudi Arabia, I knew that our family were waking up in the United Kingdom and there would be great concern if they did not hear from us. I phoned to forewarn them and to try and allay their fears, although I could only offer words of comfort and assurance with a lot of faith , which in reality was a fool`s folly. There was no answer, I would try again later.

Meanwhile on the compound Most of the wives decided to congregate into one villa, with the TV set to Sky News to see if they could gather any further information. Everyone seemed to feel safer in numbers it was only natural, a lot of their husbands had already left for work or were just about to finish their night shift it was not safe to be driving around the province at this time. I managed to meet Steve (Erica's Husband), he was one of the few men who was now locked in the compound and not at work . His wife Erica who was also a good friend was with Dawn so I could understand the sheer sense of helplessness and hell he would be feeling right now. I explained to Steve I had been in contact with Dawn and that Erica was still safe since the last time I had talked with her. Steve still hadn't heard anything from his wife so it was good to hear that Erica was up until this moment unharmed. I invited him to join everyone as a group, but he felt more secure with his emotions alone, as he did for the rest of the day.

Dave had joined the group of residents that had gathered together in one villa. The room was full of mobile phones on charge, everyone on tender hooks awaiting calls from their husbands who were still on lockdown at work. The compound shop had soon emptied its supply of phone cards and food supplies they were being bought up very quickly .

Back at the Oasis Compound..... I could hear the sound of gunfire in the distance, along with the sound of emergency sirens and helicopters flying about. Everyone was listening carefully and atentively to see if the sounds of gunfire were getting closer.

We carried on running and hurrying past the rooms and corridors looking for a safe place to take refuge. Where would it be safe? We carried on up to the second floor and found the Monday morning conference room, as we opened the door I could see another door to the rear of the room. We opened the door and closed it behind us quickly. At least we had found somewhere to hide it had felt like forever looking. At the front of the room there were three large tall black leather chairs against the wall. In the middle of the room there was a large marble table with twelve chairs. It looked exactly like a court room it felt like judgement day here. The other side of the room had a small window with a net curtain over it, underneath the window was a small desk with a small waste paper bin . By now we had gathered into a large crowd, there were about twenty-one of us, seven of the nursery staff and the rest were made up of hotel staff they were a mixture of Filipinos and Indians. Everyone found somewhere to sit. As soon as the door was closed there was an eerie feeling in the room a silence I couldn't explain. People were huddled and lined around the walls of the room. We all decided it would be a good idea to push something up against the door, the marble table was far too heavy to move. We gathered some heavy chairs and pushed them up against the door. I don't know what use it was going to be but we had to try something? We talked about turning off the lights as at the back of the room was a window which overlooked onto the passageway. If someone were to walk pass they could not see us inside if the light was off, but we could see the light their side. Jo, Erica, Julie, Margaret, Lillian, Pauline and myself found a place under the table. I found it a bit uncomfortable as I was pretty big for four and half months pregnant. Kathy climbed underneath the desk . We turned out all the lights in the room and lay very very quiet. You could hear the odd cough or sneeze and would jump when it happened.

Every single person in the room was listening attentively we were all just waiting for something to happen..... Sometimes we could hear voices and footsteps outside of the room and just about make out somebody whispering, which was frightening as I thought we had been found and the terrorists would inevitably attack us. By now the firing was getting worse outside and you could hear the faint sound of a helicopter hovering over the hotel. I could hear explosions in the distance. Would they find us? Everyone was asking each other "Are you ok don't worry we will get out of here". Erica turned to me and said "I need to ring Steve, I didn't get the chance I just need to talk with him and James my son to tell him we are ok". I felt so cruel and told Erica we couldn't use our phones incase our mobile phones would set a bomb off or a booby trap who knows I was no expert but someone had mentioned it to me earlier of the dangers. Who was I to tell Erica that she couldn't ring her husband but she knew it was right and reluctantly looked up at me and placed her phone down on the floor. Jo picked up the landline phone and started dialing through to the reception and was trying to get through to Dave the security man, he was responsible for the compound. Jo tried several times to call the reception... Jo whispered down the phone "hello, hello", she had to be so careful that the terrorists were not on the other end of the phone, but how else could we inform Dave where we were? At least this way they could try and reach us when everything was safe to do so... "We are in the Monday morning conference room there are 21 of us",(Out of the 21 the majority were of Indian origin and a few Filipino men , mainly cooks and general staff). Jo wasn't quite sure who she was talking to but was trying her best. I turned to her and said she was doing a good job and that I am sure we will all get out safe I had to convince myself otherwise . I was trying my best to stay positive. The feeling of helplessness was kicking in fast.

Jo broke down crying "I have three children what's going to happen to them I am their mother……….." Jo put her head in her hands, and started to cry.

I couldn't bear seeing Jo crying this was so cruel she was the Director of the learning centre and was normally such a strong minded lady I absolutely adored her! A really good friend .How dare the terrorists put us all through so much pain and anxiety! Our husbands and family must be so worried beyond belief about us all especially not hearing from us for a while, it was such cruelty. It must have been about two and half hours since I last called David. I started to feel a very large sense of anger coming over me . Was Ben ok in school? Had the compounds been attacked.

As I lay there, I was unaware that the schools were organizing buses with special officers from each compound to accompany the children home . What a worry it must have been for the parents wondering if the buses would be attacked and this morning just that had happened to a small school bus carrying Saudi children to school near the rainbow roundabout. Early afternoon between 12.30 and 1.30 gunfire was heard and emergency vehicles were sent to check for any casualties. Ben had also left for school that morning; it was a good 20 minutes journey to school. Ben had been informed by one of his classmates that we were still inside the compound. On entering the headmaster's office he was told not to make a scene in front of his other classmates as it could stir up panic throughout the school. Whoever had told my son this had obviously never had children! The children would unable to leave the school until it was deemed safe to do so.

Ben confided in a few friends he could trust., He had so much anxiety, the worry was building up inside him very quickly and he was trying his best not to fall apart. Ben had many friends of all nationalities. I knew his friends would comfort him after such dreadful news .

All I could think of was the last time I saw Ben. It was the night beforehand he had been arranging to go to Bahrain in a few weeks' time with our neighbour, to support him doing a gig they had planned. He had bought some new clothes; a very smart shirt and a pair of black trousers. Ben walked down the stairs of the villa and looked so handsome with his dark hair and gorgeous brown eyes; I was so very proud of him. All I could think about now was that last image of him. Would it be my last?

When you are in a situation like this you look deep into your mind, thinking and seeing the last things you said or did with your family. It was like fast forwarding your life visually in five minutes. Somehow, I felt it was so very important for me to remember every last detail. You want to tell them how very special they all are. I had always told my children how much I loved them and my husband, so I knew they would know, but it felt so very important to be able to have one more chance to say it now. I felt the tears prick, but I held the tears back; I didn't want to worry the other women with me falling apart in front of their eyes. They were all being so kind to me and concerned about my pregnancy; they were trying their best to make sure I was as comfortable as I could possibly be under the stressful and frightening circumstances.

There was an eerie silence in the room, we had already been here in this room for two hours now, but it felt like two days... Every sound or whisper was making us all very nervous and jumpy. We were not able to use a bathroom, so I was limited unfortunately to using the waste paper bins . Being pregnant and nerves kicking in, it was becoming a habit! As I looked around the room all the Indian workers were sitting with their backs against the wall, a few by now had fallen asleep and were snoring! I found this very hard to believe. Directly in front of the marble table, underneath which I was hiding, were three black tall leather chairs; it felt like judgement day. I crawled out from under the table and stood up - I couldn't take it anymore; it was so uncomfortable. My feelings now had turned from fear to anger. If I was to be killed today in cold blood I didn't want to hide from my killer. I wanted to look them straight in the eye!, By now I was exhausted by thinking too much and had decided to stand up. I quietly walked around the room . There was one glass on the refreshments tray; I took the jug of water and passed it around the room, refilling the glass making sure everyone was rehydrating . Everyone said thank you. I smiled and kept on going; it gave me a sense of strength and fulfillment that I was trying to help these frightened confused people myself included!

The noises from outside were still audible and I could hear the faint sounds of gunfire. I decided to retreat back to my safe haven under the marble table to take refuge.

Kathy was hiding underneath the desk, frightened to make a sound; she seemed frozen there. , Above her was a large window with a net curtain over it. There was a light on in the room outside so it was easy to see if anyone entered the room the other side of the window, as we had turned all the lights out in our room. It was so frightening to think someone could walk past the window at any minute and try and enter into the room we were in.

I prayed that someone was planning to rescue us - of course they were surely? I was getting very anxious again: the baby was moving and I couldn't stop shaking with the anxiety of it all., I tried to take a few deep breaths, it seemed to work…. Was my baby going to be okay? My friends turned to me and asked if I was okay and jokingly said "don't give birth now Dawn, will you!" I had visions of biting the marble table and having my baby in this very room! If I did go into labour, at least most of my friends here with me were nurses; I didn't fancy the idea though!

Another hour or two had passed and the sounds from outside seemed to be wearing off a little.

We were all restless and just wanted to go home. The morning had been long and drawn; I was very tired and exhausted, wondering if the terrorists would barge through the door at any minute and kill us all. How would they do it? I Just hoped and prayed that it would all stop very soon and that we could all go home .

Knock...knock...knock.... There here was a deadly silence in the room... Oh no! Oh God they had come for us! The silence in the room lasted for a few more minutes. Surely if it was our rescuers then they would say something? I could hear running outside, whoever it was had (thankfully) decided to give up and move on onto the next part of the building. . How lucky were we? , I was now determined, more than ever, to survive this., I just wanted to see my family again and tell them how much I loved them. I just wanted to be safe. Please, please get me out of here! I started to pray in silence . "Please lord if I have ever done anything so wrong in my life forgive me now. Can I please have another try of my life, my family, my beautiful world. I swear I will try to always be happy and help others. Please …Amen".

About forty five minutes had now passed since the knock on the door and there was now another knock.. "Hello" a voice called this time. "Is anyone there. Hello". We were all too scared to answer., Then Dave the security guard who we all knew and trusted, said, "It's okay we have come to get you out of here." I couldn't believe my ears! We were going to be rescued! The adrenalin was setting in. My prayers had been answered.,

Thank you, thank you! Everyone sat up in the room astonished;. we were not expecting this, not after so many hours of hiding away. Dave was accompanied by two special soldiers and their commander. I was rather shocked at how the commander was dressed: he had a long white thobe (typical Saudi attire - a long white buttoned shirt to the floor), a flak jacket and a motorbike helmet! "You there!". I turned around - was he talking to me? "Yes you, you first, you have a baby, Come on! Madam please!". I couldn't possibly go first I thought; I am too frightened to move., This room had been my safe haven for the last few hours . "No no, I can't you're the target not me I replied". Julie shouted, "I will go first. It's okay, come on let's get out of here." All the nursery workers including myself got up and lined up by the door - there were ten of us. The adrenalin was kicking in now:, we were going to get out of here! But, what about the others? "Please" I turned to the soldier "what about the other people -

the Indian workers and Filipinos?" It didn't feel right to leave anyone behind. Why couldn't we all leave together? It seemed so unfair to just walk away and leave them there. We were told they were to stay in the room until we had been safely evacuated from the building first. I took one last look at the remaining people left behind and couldn't help but feel saddened; I hoped someone would come back for them soon. I smiled and said goodbye and headed towards the door.

I stepped outside the door and began to shake uncontrollably as I didn't know what to expect. ,The soldier headed his way down the long corridor until we came to the top of the stairs. By now I was looking all around me suspicious of everything and everyone. The hotels interior was hardly recognizable in places; there was broken glass and bloodstains all down the walls. The terrorists had actually passed us on their way through the hotel. The whispering we had heard was them! How lucky were we that we hadn't been found?. I now tried not to look around too much and to just focus on moving forward. "Have all the terrorists been killed or have they escaped?" I asked. The soldier raised his arm and put his fingers to his lips hinting to me to be quiet . Were they still in the building? I didn't want to move let alone take another step down the marble steps . My legs started to feel like jelly. I thought I was going to pass out, I felt so vulnerable. What if they hadn't left? I couldn't think straight. I couldn't move. We slowly moved down the steps one by one, each time the soldier looked all around and had his gun ready just in case. Finally, we got down to the kitchen area. The soldier asked us to line up in twos as it would be easier and quicker to exit the building. The soldier turned his gun and pulled it tightly against his chest as if to aim; he had heard some movement coming from behind the large fridge in the kitchen. Heidi, Fin and Mackenzie came running out from behind the fridge They had been hiding there for hours. Heidi came to the learning centre everyday with Fin and Mckenzie , they were Danish and lived on the compound. Earlier in the day Heidi had arrived a few minutes after we had left the learning centre to find nobody there, she hadn't realized what was going on. She had been on her way over to the school, when suddenly, her friend Debbie, who was ahead of her on a bicycle, was shot at by a sniper on the roof! Debbie's leg had been blown off and to Heidi's horror, her children had witnessed this. Fin, her little boy was only three years old, and Mckenzie, her little girl. was just five years old. God knows how awful this must have been for the little ones- too young to witness such horror To Heidi's relief, she and her children were able to join us in the line-up.

"Okay, listen everyone to what I am about to tell you; it is very important", said the soldier. "This is the only way out of the building. There is no other way out of here safely. You will follow me and walk through that door over there - it leads to the back entrance of the kitchen. This is the only safe way out of here right now. What you are about to witness is not a very nice sight, but you must be strong and just carry on as quickly and as fast as you can. I must warn you that a man has been shot and he is dead. There is nothing we can do for him now. I am sorry but we must try and help you all to escape. Do you understand what I am telling you?. This is it: are you ready?"

Erica turned to me in a panic, "Dawn, I have a problem. I can't leave! My shoes, my shoes! I have lost my shoes,". I tried to reassure Erica she would be okay and she just needed to carry on and get herself out of here. I promised her that I would be right behind her. Our survival instincts plus panic had set in; we started to move forward – some of us reluctantly but all realizing that we has to keep going. Hopefully, freedom was on the other side of that doorway. We owed it to our families and and to ourselves to keep moving . Within seconds we had entered the back of the kitchen where the walls were covered with blood and flesh – still slowly sliding down the walls I couldn't help but look around the room, to every corner.. What had happened in here? On the floor was a body which had been covered with a white sheet. We hurried along. I tried not to look down as the scene was distressing; it brought it all back - what we had all been involved in. The dead and wounded could have been any one of us.. At last, we stepped outside. Freedom seemed so close a step away a breath away; just a little further and we could all be out of here. I looked up and could see the buildings clearly above me.   The terrorists could still be on the rooftops and easily take a shot at any of us at any moment. We climbed up the ramp and onto the side of the street. Ahead of me was a row of bollards and I could see the gate. The gate! We were nearly out! "Quickly, Quickly!" The soldier whispered. "All of you now follow me. We haven't time to stop. We must get to safety. Every second counts. Understand?" We hurried along the street looking around us all the time. We finally reached some large concrete bollards. Bollards were in place around all the compounds in the province; it was a security measure. Some of the ladies climbed over the bollards to the other side. They were free! I couldn't believe it, it was so emotional. I came to a complete stop I couldn't move. The bollards were too high for me to climb. I paused for a moment...It was just too high. Just then, I felt a sharp kick from inside of me; it was Jacob!, It was as if he was telling me to go forward ... go on mum climb. Do it for us! I stepped forward...The soldier kindly lifted me over to the other side of the bollard which was very kind as men are not supposed to touch women who are not their wives, sisters or mothers, in Saudi Arabia. But this was different; this was kindness first, regardless of rules and religions.

The streets were lined with Saudi onlookers, witnessing the shooting and crossfire of the soldiers. All the spectators looked shocked and confused; disbelief that this was happening in their province.

Chapter 3

Adorning the streets were Humvee tanks, Ambulances and Police vehicles. We kept on moving until the soldiers brought us to an empty humvee tank. We were still not safe as the firing could start again at any minute. We carried on moving forward, still in shock that this was really happening to us. I couldn't believe there were so many people looking around, watching. Weren't they afraid for themselves; that they too could get shot? Maybe the onlookers didn't believe what was happening either. We were now on the outside of the compound, but it still didn't feel very safe; we needed to be further away. not still in the line of fire.

Suddenly, a voice called out, "Inside quick, madam". I was helped up into the Humvee. It was a bit of a struggle, but I managed to do it. There were no windows, just two small slits big enough to put a gun through. I'd imagined a humvee tank to be a lot bigger than it was inside, but then I never thought I would actually ever step inside one. Why would I? At the back of the humvee sat a very young looking Saudi soldier, all kitted up and armed with a machine gun. The rest of my friends made their way into the tank and we all huddled together, shifting along to squeeze us all in. There wasn't much room, but at least we were safe. Crack! The soldiers gun went off right next to me, Luckily he had been holding his gun in an upright position; a small hole appeared in the roof. The soldier was shaking from head to toe he must have only been in his early twenties. I couldn't believe it. We had just been rescued safely from the compound full of terrorists and yet very nearly shot by friendly fire! I looked at the soldier's gun, then across at Julie, who was sitting opposite me. "Julie do you know how to use one of those things?" "I will have a bloody good go if I have to," she replied..

Where were they going to take us? Why weren't we moving? I still didn't trust anyone. No sooner had we started to move, when we stopped again. The doors to the side of the tank opened, and we could see that the crowds of onlookers had grown into a very large group. A voice spoke, "Hello everyone. I am the commander in charge of this operation. Can you answer a few questions please". I didn't want to hang around anymore, my sense of survival had kicked in more than once today and I just wanted to keep moving– to get home to my family. "Did anyone see what happened?" he continued. I plucked up the courage to reply. "Yes, the first lot of terrorists I had seen were wearing bandanas, tied around their heads. They wore flak jackets and a similar uniform to that of your soldiers." I didn't know if it had helped the commander or not, but there were no more questions and just as quickly as he appeared, he left.. Ten minutes had past and the door of the humvee opened once again.

A soldier appeared wearing a helmet which had a plastic visor attached to it. He began to count us all.

"You all have to leave this vehicle now, please," he instructed. Where were we going now I wondered? What plans did they for us? I'd half expected to see my husband outside, I was so desperate to see him, but I was trying to be strong, to keep holding on. I did believe that somehow I would see him again. It was my will and it had given me the strength to survive; to get me through the next steps of my incredible emotional and physical journey. Nobody was being allowed off the compounds around the province unless they had a very good reason too - this was obviously for their own safety. I was helped out of the humvee tank by one of the soldiers. There was a mass of police and military vehicles all around. I couldn't quite make out where I was, but by the time we were all out of the vehicle we were being led to an ambulance only a short distance away. The ambulance doors opened and the medical staff asked us to step inside. The floors were covered in blood – the blood of the injured and dead who weren't lucky enough to have escape the terror. I was reluctant to get into the ambulance, as I once again, didn't trust anyone. We were then told to get in. We just wanted to be safe and get as far away from Oasis compound as we could. "Where are we all going?", we questioned the soldier in charge. We found it all very confusing and unorganised.

"You will be taken to a safe house nearby," he replied. I was so glad to be out of Oasis compound, but still frightened, as I didn't know where we were being taken to, and was afraid we would be caught out again in the crossfire. I could still hear the firing coming from Oasis. No sooner had we driven off, the ambulance had stopped and we arrived at Saad's residence. In Saudi Arabia all residences were hidden with large walls for privacy. Saad was the owner of the Oasis resort and as you can imagine, his residence was palatial; the grounds had large gardens and huge ornamental fountains, well protected from onlookers outside. I had never had the opportunity to go inside one of these beautiful buildings before. We stepped out of the vehicle and made our way up the long path towards the large wooden doors. The doors opened and I could see a lady with her arms wide open, ready to greet us. She was dressed in the typical attire worn by Saudi women. She wore a black abaya dress and headscarf – although her abaya was a bit more luxurious; a long dark black sateen robe adorned in places with sequins and jewels. "My "baby, my baby," she called out with her arms wide open. I looked all around. Was she talking to me? Yes she was! This lovely lady approached me and put her arms around me., it was such a warm welcome and totally unexpected from a stranger, really. She instantly made me feel safe; I so needed a hug right then. What a wonderful, kind lady. The doors were closed behind us as soon as we were inside and secured and bolted. She then snapped her fingers and ordered her personal nurses to check me over. They came running into the room from different doors. I sat down on the large sofa. They checked my blood pressure and assured me, that although my blood pressure was up a little, this was to be expected and normal under the circumstances. The room was enormous and furnished with the finest furniture I had ever seen. In the centre of the room was a glass dome, decorated with tropical birds, which had many colours. It was beautiful. I couldn't take my eyes off it. I was still in shock that we were finally out of the conference room where we had been holed up for such a long time. There was a time when I had started to lose hope and thought that would die there. I was still staring up towards the glass dome; I kept wondering, what if the dome was to get hit by the gunfire? Although we were now in relative safety, we were still close to the main Oasis compound. We had only driven about five minutes away from the compound. The room started filling up with maids, all so very kind to us, offering us refreshments. Much to my delight a large tray of Patchi handmade chocolates was presented before us. Each one individually wrapped perfectly. The previous day I'd had my hospital appointment with the doctor, to check on my growing baby. Everything was going well, but I had put on an excessive amount of weight in just a few weeks, through eating those same luxury chocolates! I took a handful, not feeling guilty one bit I could just see David looking at me with his knowing grin: "Dawn, you shouldn't!". In the middle of the room a few toys were scattered, where the children of the house were playing., Fin and Mckenzie, joined in with the play. It was good to see them playing again. Poor children. I wondered what they must be thinking. It felt very homely, here in Al Saad's palace. We were all grateful to have our minds taken off the recent events. A little bit of normality felt so good.

I reached for my phone; it had been hours since I had last talked with David and I knew that he would have been frantic with worry. The adrenalin ran through my body again. I dialled the number, anxiously waiting to hear David's voice again... "David, I'm okay! We are all okay! Oh I love you so much. I can't tell you how good it is to hear your voice again, I thought the last time I called you that was it! I think everything is going to be okay now, but I won't be right until I get out of this safe house".

"What safe house?" David enquired. "Dawn it is wonderful to hear you are in a safe place". It must have been very distressing for him, not knowing where I was and trying to fill in the gaps of my day. I explained to him that we had all been taken in an ambulance to Saad's residence, that it wasn't too far away from the Oasis compound, but at least we were all out of there. "Is Ben okay? Is he home yet?"

"Yes, he is fine, Dawn," David replied, "He has been so worried about you, they are getting security to go up to the school and he should be back on the compound very soon".

When it was safe to do so, the children were escorted from their school, back to their family compounds, by the compound's security officer. Can you imagine how those children must have felt - the emotion, the fear, on their return journey home? When Ben reached Las Dunas compound gates, David was there, waiting to meet him off the school bus. The feeling of relief for both of them was enormous.

I didn't like the thought of Ben travelling on the roads as anything could happen, "I have to go now, sorry, as my phone battery is nearly dead, so I must save it for further calls to you when I can., I will try and find a charger when I can. I love you".
"I love you too Dawn, take care please darling!"

I tried to call my daughter Aimee but couldn't get a reply, I hadn't talked with her yet and I really needed to. I switched my phone off.

An hour had passed and the doors had been opening and closing within this time as more people had been rescued from the Oasis Compound. There must of been about a hundred people in the room; it was getting rather crowded now and I was getting rather concerned about the glass dome above me. In my mind I was thinking of every possible thing that could happen: ways in which the gunmen could break into the house and find us. My mind was working overtime, but I was not surprised; when something like this happens to you, it is just so unbelievable, but you carry on and try to stay positive , survive the best you can and plan ahead to protect yourself.

The lady of the house looking up at the dome with great concern and asked if we would like to go upstairs, as this would be a bit more comfortable and quieter for us. My friends and I made our way upstairs where we found a living room a lot smaller than the one we were previously in. I preferred it here as it felt more homely. Looking around, there were several sofas dotted around the room, a tv to the side and a large coffee table situated in the middle. As soon as I found a place on the sofa, I decided to try calling my daughter, Aimee, again. Aimee was living in the UK and it was always so hard saying goodbye after our visits, waiting for the long stretches to pass until we had enough holiday to go home and see her again. I didn't want to upset or worry her, but I needed to hear her voice. I dialled her number and waited anxiously. "Aimee? Hello darling ," I could not disguise the anxiety in my voice.

"Mum? Are you okay?"

"Aimee, my love, I have been involved in a terrorist attack at the Oasis Compound. I can't go into detail now as I have a low battery. I am just so glad I am able to talk with you. I can't believe this has all happened and I am amazed and shocked by it all; it's been my worst nightmare, that's all I can say."

I took a deep breath as once again, I needed to tell my daughter how much she meant to me, "Please listen to me lovely, if anything should happen to me, you do know I love you so very much. I just need you to know this". Aimee was very quiet. It wasn't the normal conversation you would have with your daughter and obviously she was upset at hearing such awful news. It was hard for her to take in. "Oh mum, I know you love me. Please take care mum. I love you so much ".

I fought back the tears. I had to be strong, I didn't want Aimee to remember me crying. I know I was in the 'safe house' but I didn't feel very safe. The only place I would feel safe right now was at home, with all my family together. "Bye for now darling. Ring dad, he can fill you in with what has been going on. I love you so much bye".

Earlier in the day.....

Mags, Alison and Jane, friends of mine on Las Dunas compound, worked at the Redwood Nursery on the Al Hada Compound. They had left Las Dunas on the compound bus as normal, with some of the other residents' children - Jodie, Georgia and Rebecca who attended the nursery. When they arrived Al Hada Compound, they immediately thought something was wrong, as the guards were looking at them strangely, as if they shouldn't have been there. They usually arrived at Al Hada around 8.15 a.m. A few of the parents on the Al Hada compound came over to the nursery building to tell them something was going on and that they were keeping their children at home. The British Consulate was across the road from the Al Hada Compound, so they may have got warned early on.! Alison then called the gatehouse to find out more and to double-check what she had been told by the residents. It was confirmed. Al Hada was now in lockdown, and no one would be able to leave the compound until further notice. Jane called the Dhahran British Grammar School where her two boys, Christopher and Johnathan attended school (the same school as my Ben). Jane couldn't get through as the lines were extremely busy with concerned parents calling. Jane's husband, Taz, called around in work to see if they could gather any more information about the school. Luckily, the boys were safe and everything was okay - much to Jane's relief as she couldn't get off Al Hada Compound for the time being. Jane was in touch with the school for most of the day making sure and through a lot of shouting that there had been no changes to the security of her children. She also wanted to find out when her boys would be brought back safely to their compound.

The children who attended the nursery school on Al Hada, were of different nationalities, living elsewhere around the Province. As some children had already arrived at the nursery, they were now locked-down on the compound, with no details of when they could go home. As the news spread externally, parents were obviously extremely distraught to realise that their children were caught up in a terrorist situation which was going on around the area of their nursery. Mags had taken a call from a concerned mother, crying down the phone, fearful for her child. Mags reassured her that she and the other nursery staff would do everything they could to safeguard her child and that they would not abandon her child under any circumstances. It was a very emotional moment: the gravity of the situation and the enormity of the responsibility.

A few of the residents on Al Hada phoned the nursery to say they were going to send food over if they could , but that they were afraid to come out of their homes even though they were inside the compound along with the nursery building. The children who were already at the nursery were too young to be aware of what was going on around them.. Mags, Jane and Alison tried to keep the children all amused the best they could, whilst taking it in turns to phone friends to try and get updates on the situation outside. . At around 4 pm , Jed, the father of Georgia, one of the Las Dunas children, who was at the nursery with Mags, Jane and Alison, phoned to say he was coming to pick everyone up. Ged had to shout at the security guards on Las Dunas to convince then to let him leave the compound to go and get his daughter. No buses were authorised to leave the compounds. No one knew if they really had permission to be on the streets at this time but the security guards on Las Dunas let him out. Each compound in Dhahran had guards on the front gates and concrete chicanes were placed in front of guard houses to stop anyone ramming their way in with a car. Gunfire had been heard at the neighbouring supermarket, Giant Stores, so it was risky to venture outside, but some families on Las Dunas had not been able to see their children since before 8am that morning, so it was hard for them to sit around just waiting. It had gone quiet in the afternoon and the Al Hada guards had allowed some parents to collect their children from the nursery, so when Ged came for Mags, Jane, Alison and the three children, they moved quickly to get back to their own compound and their own families. It was only a short ride back to Las Dunas, and Ged took a route away from the main road where Oasis was and the roadblocks were set up, but everyone was still apprehensive. All the roads around the area were eerily quiet. Once back at Las Dunas, Mags, Jane and Alison got caught with all the events of the day and learned that I, along with Erika from Las Dunas, were still caught up in the events and were not yet back on our own compound. When the others were safely back at the Las Dunas compound, many of the residents had started to gather on my neighbour, Lorraine's patio to hear and share any news and updates.

David's parents, Sue and Jeff, who live in the UK, had been in touch with David throughout the day. Sue couldn't bring herself to try and call me as they were so concerned about my safety they didn't want to call and get upset or put me in danger. Everyone was putting on a brave face for each other . Sue and Jeff were at the theatre with friends and were popping out every half an hour for updates from David. To be honest they really didn't want to be out socializing at a time like this but it had all been pre-arranged and so they just went ahead with the arrangements. They took it in turns to call David.

David re-joined everyone on Lorraine's patio as he was the security person for the compound and tried to keep everyone calm. Everyone was talking about the confusion of the company and the lack of official information. There had been concerns about how the compound buses had been allowed to leave in the morning after the some of the terrorist attacks had already started. Some residents felt the situation somehow could have been prevented if informed earlier. There were a lot of angry parents.

There was a scream from outside Lorraine's patio.. "Some-ones been shot!". A voice called out "come quick I can see blood and gunshot wounds!" One of the compound Indian workers had been working on the roof of one of the buildings near the main gate, which was opposite Lorraine's villa. He was lying on the ground and sounded like he was in pain. The women were in a state of panic: they thought that the terrorists were advancing towards the compound!

One of the female residents checked him over for injuries. It was nothing serious just a few bumps and bruises from falling off the roof - and no bullet wounds! Apparently, he was wearing two layers of clothing on and his undergarment was red. On top of this he wore a white t-shirt, which he had snagged during his fall. When the residents who helped him got back to Lorraine's patio and announced the story, everyone burst out laughing, seeing the funny side to the story. Everyone was relieved the at the compound wasn't under attack. Back at the safe house I had decided to have a look around the room; I needed a change of scenery. Situated to the right of me, was a bathroom., I needed to freshen up, I didn't want to cry in front of the little ones as I needed to stay strong; that's what had pulled me through this day so far - staying strong and alert for my family; having the will and determination to see them again. I entered the bathroom. The sink top was a delight: there must have been about ten bottles of the finest perfumes and lotions you could buy. I looked up at the mirror and saw my reflection. I rubbed my eyes; I couldn't believe I looked so white and so pale. It was to be expected with all the worry and it still wasn't over. I so longed to go home to see my family, to hold my husband, just to see him again. I started thinking about if we would ever get out of here. It had been such a long day...

I left the bathroom and started to walk around the rooms to get my bearings. I came across an open door and could hear voices from inside; , it was Saad's, the owner of the house, eldest daughters. They were packing several large suitcases and doing it very quickly.. I apologised for walking into the room, but they didn't seem to notice me; they were completely unaware of my presence. they were too busy trying to pack! I asked them where they were going? One of them shouted over to me, "London. We are leaving straight away for London, we will be safer there". They carried on packing and grabbing anything to hand. My mobile phone battery was so low now I was starting to worry that I wouldn't be able to keep in touch with anyone.

"Have you any chargers I could borrow please?" I asked.

"Yes", one of the girls replied, and opened one of the drawers in front of them. Fantastic! There were a variety of chargers and lots of them too. I ran back to the living room and told my friends that they should charge their phones up while we had a chance. We couldn't help but notice the breaking news on the tv, They were broadcasting about the terrorist attack on the news! It seemed surreal. We all got rather annoyed when a British expat who was being interviewed was going on about how 'us British could handle being in this situation and to keep up a stiff upper lip' over events., The cheek of it! She wouldn't be saying that if she had been in our shoes.

In the weeks leading up to the 29th May, there had been terrorist activity all over Saudi Arabia. On 1st May 2004 there was a security incident in Yanbu where a group of Arab men entered the offices of Abb Lummus and started firing at western employees. There were fatalities, two Britons, two US nationals and an Australian. A Saudi Arabian National guard was also killed along with and 19 others. One of the terrorists that was on the 'most wanted list' was also killed. Another was badly injured. As the terrorists were trying to escape, there were reports of them shooting at several shops in the vicinity.

Further attacks still carried on: on May 22nd 2004, a German national was shot dead in the Saudi capital, Riyadh, near the Jarir shopping complex. Security measures were tightened around the Western Compounds: the usual texts regarding safety procedures, alarms etc. and possible lockdowns were a reminder of action to be taken. By now patience was starting to run a bit thin and there was a sense of tension around. People on the street looked more alert and leading up to the latest attack the streets had been eerily quiet. Margaret, one of the nursery teachers in the room, had decided to call the British embassy in Saudi to see if they could help us , but as soon as she had got through she was redirected to an answerphone -

"Charming," Margaret said, annoyed. "It looks like everyone has gone and left us. Unfortunately we're going to have to fend for ourselves." We all started to wonder what to do next, who to ring and how we could get back to our compounds safely. We sat around talking to each other in disbelief on what had just happened. I think because we had stayed so quiet for so many hours it felt strange talking again. I didn't like to see my friends looking so worried; we were normally all such a happy bunch of women. We were so thankful that the children hadn't made it in to nursery school today, as it would have been even harder to keep the children quiet. They wouldn't have understood the danger. I couldn't bear the thought of anyone of them being harmed. We had later found out that the terrorists on Oasis had taken several people hostage, including a nine year old Lebanese boy and his mother and father. The terrorists had been walking around the compound and knocking on the doors of peoples' villas, asking residents if they were Muslims or Christians. If they were Muslims, they had to provide documents to prove this. If they could not supply this information then they were either beheaded or were being shot point blank in the head...

I decided to call my stepfather back home in the UK as my battery was fully charged now. I'd hoped he hadn't been watching the news. Maybe David would have already told him what had happened and that I was now relatively safe. I just wanted to reassure him and my mother; my mother was in hospital for a minor operation and was still recovering. I Just hoped I could get a hold of my stepfather at the right moment. The ringing seemed longer than usual; it was only a few minutes, but I just wanted to hear his voice. My stepfather was a kind and caring man who could always reassure me in times of need. He answered. "Dawn, Dawn is that you?" Thank heavens where are you now? Are you okay? Don't worry you will be out of there soon".

I could hear a distant cry in his voice, my stepfather never cried - he was a big softy, but never showed his emotions and I knew he would be trying hard not to upset me now. He told me that David had let him know that I been taken to a safe house. I told him what I could and reassured him that I was okay. It had been a a terrifying experience and I couldn't believe it wasn't over yet. I knew that my stepfather would obviously still be worrying and he wouldn't be okay until I returned back to the UK and he could see for himself. He told me to ring my mother as he had been on the way over to the hospital when I called. I didn't want to call and upset her, but she could have been watching the news and would be worried sick. She'd be heartbroken, so it was best to let her know as soon as I could – but also in case the situation took a turn for the worse. I needed to be able to speak one last time with my mother.

79

Although where would I start with explaining it all?

My mother was called to the ward reception desk to take my call. She was just about strong enough to walk after her operation. The nurse told her that her daughter was on the phone My mum picked up the phone, "Hello, Dawn? Is everything okay? "Hi mum, I am so sorry to tell you but I have been involved in a terrorist attack!" There was a few seconds of silence... I know mum couldn't believe what I was saying it's not the usual comment you would come out with . I could hear the phone drop..... "Dawn, oh my god are you hurt? I love you...... Where are you ? My mother's voice was a mixture of panic and fear, I could just about make out her words, her voice was trembling.

"Mum, I am out of the Oasis compound now but I am still not in the clear. I am so sorry to put you through this as you're not very well also, but I'm staying in a safehouse near the compound although we cannot be moved until it is safe. They are planning on moving and taking us back to our compounds, but I don't know when as the streets are still unsafe, and they are not very clear in what they are doing– there is a lot of confusion. I love you mum, I just wanted to tell you. Please don't worry, I am bearing up the best I can and as soon as I am out of here I will call you". I could hear my mum telling the nurses at the desk what had happened. They were clearly very concerned as mums condition was deteroriating quickly and the concern was how this shocking news could affect her. Mum said goodbye and told me to take care of myself; she was crying. My poor mum. I just wanted to hold her now. My mother left the desk and the nurses took her back to the ward where she was given some medication to calm her down; she was sedated for a while. My poor mother. I know myself how I would have been if I had had a call from one of my children with such news. I knew my stepfather would be there soon to look after her and I felt reassured knowing this. It was so very hard living away from my family, but my place was with my husband and the saying of goodbyes when back in the UK visiting everyone, was never easy. But now all I wanted to do was be with my family back home my daughter, my mum, my stepdad, my sister.

Chapter 4

I was lucky enough to have had Ben with me in Saudi for a short while, at least until he had finished his school here in Dhahran. Even to this day, Ben says living in Saudi was the best days of his life so far, as he had made many friends from different countries. We all enjoyed our time in Saudi: we belonged to a very close knit community on the Las Dunas Compound and amused ourselves by using all the facilities available. It was a bit like Marmite you either liked it or you hated it. It wasn't a life choice for everyone. Either way, you had the choice to make the best of it as you could, afterall, you were there to support your husband in his job and to be together as a family unit so the least you could do was try to adjust. That was my motto.

There was a large swimming pool on Las Dunas in the shape of a giant peanut, all designed with a Spanish feel to it with large orange and yellow villas. Apparently the owner of the compound had tried to emulate a compound in Spain, which was also called Las Dunas. We had overheard stories that the owner and his family had enjoyed holidaying there.

The restaurant and gym were frequently used by residents. The restaurant was called "Los Olivios" and had a good variety of food on the menu, and was where friends would all meet for lunch and a chat once or twice a week. It was a good way to socialise and we were thankful to meet up as you could easily become housebound and bored as many women didn't have jobs and the children were at school all day. It was a good facility to have. Sometimes functions would be held there if someone was leaving the Kingdom to return home: we called this a
Masalama Party, which means goodbye in Arabic. The women on the compound also organised craft classes to keep us busy and learn new things from each other. Once per week, we met for quilting classes. This was

good fun and amazing to see the different creations everyone would come up with. This class was very popular with the women and surprisingly a few men too!

My days were mainly taken up by my early morning gym sessions, followed by a coffee and a chat with a few ladies from the compound. I enjoyed being a lady of leisure. Midweek, a few of us ladies would venture out of the compound and take the bus to the local markets in Dammam, a town about a half an hour's drive away. We would hunt around for the 'bargain of the week', delving through the masses of shoe markets and material souks! It was like an Aladdin's Cave of junk – and treasure if you looked hard enough- but we loved the excitement of it all. A few of the ladies were well known in the material shops and we were getting very good at bartering our price. The shopkeeper enjoyed the bartering of prices too. Life here was a lot different to Britain: at home your vegetables and fruit would be neatly wrapped up and washed in a well presented tray; in Saudi, you had to rummage your way through the mounds of rotten or just edible fruit and vegetables to strike it lucky. We got accustomed to this way of life and a few of us paid for it too with stomach bugs etc. Still it was an unique way of living here and it is the way the Arabs had lived for hundreds of years, trading through their markets. I loved the bread which was still cooked in the stone kilns and had that distinct stone-baked smell and flavour. Local food could be so cheap. Rice was cooked in large cauldrons and placed in medium sized brown bags and sold for pennies!

The downside was that every woman had to be covered up in public in Saudi, regardless of your own religion or nationality. A ladies attire would consist of an Abaya: a long black gown which had to cover your ankles and wrists. If you travelled further out into the old towns it was a good idea to cover your head too so as not to offend anyone. (Basically a woman in Saudi was seen as a second class citizen). The muslim Holy Quran states that 'women cover themselves with a loose garment. They will thus be recognised and no harm will come to them'. This surely says more about the men!

A few times I had been shouted and scorned at for not covering my head.

We would sometimes stop during prayer times for a coffee , then carry on with shopping after the prayers ended. We had got used to the prayer times:, all the shops would close for 35 minutes sometimes up to an hour whilst people travelled to the mosques or prayed within their premises. Afterwards, shops reopened and shopping would resume as normal. This would happen at leasy three times during the day and early evening. How I missed England and the uninterrupted Mackenzie ate a little then sat back, oh so quietly, her mother watching intently. What she had witnessed must have been an awful and frightening experience. She was shopping habits, but in Saudi the shops opened very late in the evening so if you didn't mind going out then, you could catch up on your shopping.

A small Filipino woman entered the room with a large silver platter full of chicken nibbles, chips, hamburgers and rolls. The hospitality was overwhelming and we were all very thankful, but a few of us were sickened at what was going on and had lost their appetite. Mackenzie, one of the nursery children who had joined us in the kitchen during our escape, came and sat next to me. I tried to get her to eat something as to her mother's dismay she hadn't touched anything since the morning. She was only five years old. Heidi looked at me and said, "Dawn, I am so worried she will remember what she saw this morning". I tried my best to give her some hope. I told her that children do forget things and if lucky she might erase it all from her memory. I prayed she would forget. I started reciting Goldilocks and the Three Bears to Mackenzie, to keep her calm and to keep her focused on something else: the poor child. Mackenzie looked like Goldilocks, she had white-blonde hair and big blue eyes., Her younger brother Fin was exactly the same. They were from Denmark and a real pleasure to have at the nursery. Heidi and Albert, their parents, were always so pleasant when dropping their children off at the school. We reached the part of the story where daddy bear asks, "whose been sleeping in my bed?" - Mackenzie sat up, "I want to talk to my daddy! I want to talk to my daddy!". Albert her father, was not available to talk to at this time. "Mckenzie, would you like to talk to my daddy?" I asked her. It was the best I could do right now. "Yes". I called my father but got no answer, so I decided to call David instead. David answered the phone and I explained what I needed from him and he talked to

Mackenzie for a short while. Between us, we both talked about the Goldilocks story, and gradually we had one little frightened girl starting to smile - something I thought might not happen for a very long time. Mackenzie said goodbye to David and soon settled down on the sofa and fell asleep. Heidi had gone downstairs to try and find out what the Saudi authorities were intending next and how and when they were going to move us but there was still no news. We didn't know that one of the other nursery teachers had been in contact with the General Manager of the province for British Aerospace Systems . This was the company my and some of the other women's husbands worked for. I wished we had known about this contact at the time as it would have helped reassure us if we had known.

To the right of me was an elevator which made me feel uneasy and very nervous. It seemed a bit odd to have an elevator adjoined to your living room but it made sense as the house was very big and I was made aware by one of the maids that the lady of the house had a disabled child. I kept imagining that the terrorists would find their way in via the elevator and the doors would burst open and we would all be killed. My mind continued to work overtime during the long wait and I could not relax.

Those poor people who were still on the Oasis Compound: all I could think about was all the others we had left behind. I hoped and prayed that they had rescued the other people we had shared so many hours with in one room. We had noticed earlier whilst watching the news that a 9 year old Lebanese boy and his parents had been taken hostage. Sky's 'breaking news' had confirmed that the boy had been released, thankfully. Within the next 30 minutes of watching him on the news, the boy arrived at our safe house; it seemed so incredible to see him on the television and then to see him join us in the safe house. I will never forget the look on that boys face: he was very pale almost white, the fear and the pain etched on his face. This poor child what had he seen? What had he witnessed? His parents were still being held by the terrorists and no one knew what would become of them. What do you say to a child who has had his parents taken away from him?, He may never see them again. Erica sat down beside him and tried her best to reassure him , trying to help take his mind off the events. He could hardly talk; he was obviously traumatized, thinking about what might become of his parents. Over the next hour or so a few more people, who had managed to escape from Oasis Compound, arrived at the safe house. Like us, they arrived looking frightened and bewildered; some were covered in blood stains and dirt from where they had tried to climb to safety . It was still hard to believe that this could be happening, that I was a part of it. I tried not to think about what they would have gone through, but I was so concerned for them – that they had experienced such terror. A little girl arrived with her family. Nova; I recognised her from attending the nursery where I worked . I felt so angry that this little girl had needed to run for her life. Her parents looked so happy and relieved to be here at the safe house. They too, were covered in blood and their clothes were torn and dirty. We offered them some food and tried to make them as comfortable as we could. We talked about what had happened to them. They told us that they had had to climb onto the roof of their villa to escape; the terrorists were going to set fire to their home and were already trying to burn people out of their homes. Thankfully they were the lucky ones. Everybody was fleeing for their lives...they were really lucky to have made it. One of the Indian workers told us that he was cleaning one of the villas, when her heard the terrorists approaching . He had managed to climb inside the air conditioning unit to take refuge where he hid for a few hours. Whilst inside the unit he witnessed some of the terrorists helping themselves to the alcoholic beverages! A variety of sweets were also consumed. As soon as they left he climbed down and hid under the bed until he was found and rescued. He was one of the lucky ones; a survivor.

From the safe house gunfire and explosions could still be heard for several hours more. The Saudi Special Forces arrived from Riyadh; they had landed on the roof of the hotel by helicopter and had surrounded the building. The gunmen on the compound were still holding people captive – still searching for the "non-believers" as they would call them. I had later found out that the two guards on the gate of Oasis, who had let us in first thing in the morning, had been shot dead. Two very brave young men, they had made an attempt to try and stop the gunmen: protecting us they gave their own lives. I owed them my life. This news was devastating; we had seen these men everyday whilst coming to work. It didn't make sense to me: fanatics wanting to kill and injure innocent people for the sake of religion.

Around 4 pm Ben had managed to get the school bus back to the compound. The school thought that everything had died down and that it was safer to go home while it was still light. The correct procedures were implemented: all the school buses were checked over, much to the relief of the many students who now had to make the anxious journey back to their residential compounds.

This journey back home to the compound was longer than usual for Ben and his fellow friends. All the children were nervously watching the roads and surrounding areas as they were bussed home. Ben had later told me that he felt that everyone on the bus was looking at him - obviously thinking about what might have happened to me, probably wondering if I still alive. Ben just stared out of the window, ignoring everything else around him. He couldn't wait to get back to Dave, where he hoped to find me also.

Finally, they reached the compound gates where anxious mums and dads were already waiting, eager to collect their children. The gates opened and David was there waiting for Ben. It was such a relief and emotional to have his son back safely in his arms again. Ben hugged his father and broke down crying, "Dad...". At last, Ben could release and give in to all his emotions safely in the arms of his father. Ben could hardly speak, the words choking him as he tried.
"It's okay Ben. It's going to be ok, I just know we will see your mother again, she is strong when she wants to be". These words of my husband would both haunt and save me years later.

Once back at the villa, Ben started to question his father about any news he may have heard, so he could build up a picture of what had happened throughout the day. "Dad have you heard from Mum at all?"

"Yes, Ben, she is okay for now, I have talked with her for a short while."

Ben sat down in the armchair in the corner of the room and looked out of the window, deep in thought. He started taking notes on how he was feeling; somehow it helped ….

Ben wrote:

Sometimes when you're deep in thought and you think what it would really be like when your parents die, but it hasn't happened, you come back to reality, so it doesn't feel too bad...

The reality of my mum dying now was so frightening and so real because it could materialise at any time. She could have been shot already and I wouldn't even know! She could have left this world. Every moment I wasn't with her seemed an eternity., I just needed to know if she was okay I needed the warmth of my mother's arms around me. Would I ever see her again? I couldn't bring myself to be around many people, so I stayed in my room out of the way, playing my guitar for a while, trying to drown out my thoughts to make the time pass . "Please come home, Why was dad being so brave? It was probably for me, clinging on to the hope that mum would return. He couldn't sit still though: pacing back and forth, keeping Mum". I allowed the tears to flow but I felt numb.

I was worried about my father's state of mind. What must it be like for him? It would be easier if I didn't let him see me cry.
Even in this 40C heat I felt cold. I thought it was the air conditioning in the villa , but It was something else.   Dark…. darkness spinning its web through my mind and soon it was the only thing I could think about.   It consumed me. "What if she's dead?" I had to use my strength to pull away from such

thoughts. Neil Una's husband good friends of our family poured me a large mug of coffee which helped Why was dad being so brave? It was probably for me, clinging on to the hope that mum would return. He couldn't sit still though: pacing back and forth, keeping busy counting the hours anything to pass the time. Another hour or two had passed and my friend, Sam called round. We sat outside on the kerb, discussing how we would like to join the army and then we could wipe out all the terrorists and get even. We walked around the compound for a while. It was eerie. Everyone was staying indoors. Before Sam left to go back to his villa he gave me a hug and shook my hand. He hoped that everything would be alright and being such a good friend, told me, "you know where I am if you need to talk".

Back in the United Kingdom, mum had gathered all her belongings together at the hospital and waited for my stepfather to pick her up. She was eager to get home now as she couldn't really talk openly about what had happened. I knew she would be trying to reach me by phone, wanting answers to her questions, but more importantly making sure I was in a safe place.. Mum always worried about us living in the Middle East, and told me this often when I visited her. Only what any mother would do though, protecting their young.

She has a picture hanging on her living room wall above the fireplace of an Arabian lady with camels and sand dunes in the background. Mum always told me she used to pretend it was me...

The day was starting to feel so long now. We were all awaiting news on when we could leave this safe house, it felt like we had been here forever! I don't think any of us thought we'd be here as many hours as we were. Some people were starting to feel let down and abandoned and were obviously curious if the officials were trying to sort something out for us sooner rather than later. We constantly asked when we would be able to and get back to our families, but all we got back was, "We are sorting it, ma'am, but we have to clear it first. We are very sorry. We're doing everything in our power to get you back home to your families." Eventually things starting to turn around: the safe house was starting to clear and it sounded a lot more quieter now. Outside, it was getting darker and I couldn't help but feel a bit anxious as to how we were going to get out of the building. One woman stood up and said,

"Right, I have had enough now. I need to leave. What is going on, please?"

We were all taken downstairs to a small room at the back entrance of the safe house. Inside the room was a young boy with his father, sitting at a table, just waiting and sitting there with a battery generated power light. They looked white and very tired. What was the plan? How were we all going to be rescued? All I could hear in the room was the chitter chatter about how the Saudi special forces were going to storm the building later and that they had already arrived by helicopter and were taking their positions. Were they going to storm the building while we were still here? I started to feel really unsafe and very frightened once again. The tension in the room rose. Jo shouted at the man in charge of holding us here. He was accountable for us.

"I can't believe it? Where has everybody gone?" shrieked Jo. "Ma'am. please we are trying." "Even the cats have left the building!" Jo said angrily. I didn't blame her, feeling like this, it seemed as though we were the last few people left and that they had given up on us. Julie had managed to get the General Manager of our husbands' Company on the phone, so I asked to talk to him. He was responsible for all our safety whilst working and living in the Kingdom. Julie passed me the phone,

"Dawn, listen, I know you are all eager to get out of there. We have been trying our best to return you safely. We understand what an awful ordeal it must have been -and still is horrific for you all -. We have to follow certain rules and procedures before coming to rescue you as we have a duty of care and responsibility for you all. We have to play it by the book."

When you are in a situation like this rules mean nothing. You live for the moment and grasp any chance of freedom you can take. .

"Dawn we are sending a bus to come and collect you all very soon. The bus is to take you to the Intercontinental Hotel, where we will all be waiting to meet you all, including your husbands. Just hold on a little longer. It won't be too much longer now, I promise you. We nearly have the clearance we need".

I couldn't believe what I was hearing! The adrenalin rushed and kicked in all the way through my body. We were finally going to get out. We were going to be okay. Can you imagine how we all felt at this moment? The thought of freedom, our families. We were not going to be harmed. I felt so safe and reassured. Our prayers had been answered. I turned to my friends and shared the wonderful news with them.

I will never forget the smiles on my friends' faces: the look of relief, the happiness and the sheer delight. We were going home. Home!
It was a little while before we were told to get ready to get on the bus . Still in shock at the actual possibility of getting out of here I looked all around me to take one last look at where we had been for the past ten or so hours, I was thankful for the kindness and the hospitality of Saad's family of taking care of us and allowing us into their home to take shelter. I was so   excited, emotional, and truly estatic to know I would see my family again. All I could think of now was David safe travelling to the hotel ? Were the roads safe to drive on?
We all headed towards the doorway none of us knowing what to expect outside these

doors. I buttoned up my Abaya and took a deep breath.......

We stepped outside, I never looked back again......................

The air was warm and dusty but freedom was just around the corner and felt and smelt so good. It was very dark outside, I turned to Erica and said " lets walk slowly and be very careful ". As we tiptoed and headed out into towards the garden our backs were arched as if hiding away from the gunmen. We were still very unsure if we were safe but a few more steps and we would be on the bus on our way to our loved ones . We huddled our way through the garden in and out of the bushes being very aware of our surroundings. Finally all the ladies got onto the bus, some took their seats but most of us lay down in the aisle of the bus. We all turned to each other and formed a human chain linking one another's hands together and squeezed them tightly. We were still frightened , this proved to me how much we had been terrorised today but there was hope it was happening , this was the moment this was our time, our freedom, everything we had prayed for, this moment was priceless.

All my colleagues would hold a special place in my heart I would never forget what we had all been through this day. The bus moved onto the highway and we made our way down the main road. I was very scared we would be shot at again I thought I may not ever be mentally okay again . How will I overcome today? It was too early to assess my psychological state now all I wanted was David now and my family.

I started imagining everyone standing in the hotel awaiting our arrival and how very emotional it would be . It hadn't seemed that long before we arrived at the hotel. he bus pulled outside the hotel, we all moved forward keen to exit the bus knowing our loved ones were in the hotel . I headed my way towards the main door of the hotel.

People were running back and for looking for their loved ones…..I suddenly stopped and for a moment I felt like I was the only person in the room , if you can imagine that you are in a room and everyone is talking but you don't hear a thing , it's as if you are so enthralled in what your doing you block it out. I looked around again and To the left of me my friends husband spotted his wife and ran forward to greet her with open arms . The tears great emotions were flowing . I was starting to come back to reality now and I could hear the sobbing and the chatter in the room . I was still lost and alone in this room looking around for David. The General Manager of the province was here also with his wife . I looked around the room directly in front of me staring at me was David!!! David ran towards me with open arms and with a huge smile on his face the look I had imagined I would see again and hoped for. We fell into each other's arms and David held me like he had never held me in all his life." Oh god

Dawn I love you " I was so worried I was going to lose you, your safe now let me take you home to your family . It felt so lovely being back in the arms of my loved one . Everyone was holding each other close and comforting one another. The General manager and his wife made their way around the room asking each one of us were we okay and if there was anything they could do to help any of us. I just wanted to get back to the compound now to see Ben to hold him and tell him it was going to be okay to tell him how much I loved him. I felt so fortunate to be alive to be able to stand tall and not hide away. I still couldn't help but think what had happened to the other people we had left in the room , surely they would have been rescued by now?. David was telling me how quiet the roads were still and how people had preferred to stay on their compounds as a lot of people were still afraid to travel outside due to the terrorist activity. I knew due to today's events a lot of people would be leaving the kingdom of Saudi Arabia as it would of made them very frightened for safety and family.

I quickly said goodbye to my friends and in a funny way I felt strange leaving these friends of mine as we had been through a lot together emotionally and physically . I was so very happy to see the smiles on their faces now being reunited again with their loved ones it was an unforgettable moment. I headed towards our car outside. Taking a look back towards the Oasis compound it was just a meer shadow in the distance now. I don't think I could ever go back there I thought to myself. I had some good memories to take with me.

Chapter 5

We were nearly back at Las Dunas and I knew all my friends would be so glad to see us all return safely . We pulled up at the checkpoint and showed our passes to the gates security. The security men were thoroughly checking the car at the same time they were nervously looking all around. The gates of Las Dunas opened something I had visualized happening all day and returning home. I had a huge lump sitting in my throat. It felt unreal I was nearly home. All I could think about now was Ben. The streets were very quiet on the compound. David pulled up and stopped halfway up the street , in the distance I could make out a figure... it was Ben he had been waiting eagerly for our return. My heart filled with excitement a rush that I can only explain to any other mother she feels when her child may have been in danger. I leapt out of the car and started running towards Ben with every breath I took I was choking with the emotion, Ben fell into my arms. "Ben ! " "Oh thank god I can hold you lovely" "Are you ok"? All I could hear was bens tears of relief and joy my child was back in my arms how lucky I felt to hold him again.

I thanked Una and Neil for looking after Ben . We made our way back to our villa. I didn't really feel like seeing anyone right now . I just needed to be on my own. The events of today were a lot to take in. It still all felt surreal. It was too early to talk with anyone right now, I just wanted to bury my head into a pillow and scream and cry with relief! It was something that would affect me for the rest of my life .

There was an incoming call... it was my dad, it was dad!..."I have got her Ben!"

Una opened the front door and I stepped outside. I looked left on the road and I saw a brown car and realised it was my dad's. It was at the bottom of the road and it came up and stopped About 50 metres away from me. Somebody got out, I could see it was my mother, it was unreal at first because of the whole picture I had unintentionally and unavoidably created in my thoughts was running through my head from the moment I was told by my school mates this morning. My mother jumped out of the car because she didn't want to wait any longer to see me. She and I both ran and we met in the middle of the road. We held each other and the only way I can explain It was a release from the cold grips of death's plan that had so eagerly and joyfully held on to my consciousness. She was home and I'd never been so happy to hold her in all my life, the world had given her back to me and I never wanted to let go again............

Still even today after all these years these words of my son bring a tear to my eye its knowing how much I mean to him and how much I love him too, the words of love are very touching . The phone call to my daughter reassuring her I was okay, hearing the anxiety in her voice will stay with me forever.

We headed our way home, yes home ,where I had dreamed and prayed of coming back to as a family again. I stepped inside our villa closed the door and never wanted to leave again. I sat down on the settee and hugged Ben and David until I fell asleep the relief the exhaustion was overwhelming me, nothing else mattered we were together again. I was happy to have made it home in the arms of my loved ones . I slept all night undisturbed surprisingly I was so glad to be home.

In the afternoon the compound doctor held a surgery at our villa as he felt it was more convenient to all concerned to gather here and it was more informal. The debriefing by the doctor was held one by one in my kitchen. We were glad of the visit as we were very distressed and wondered why the company had not bothered to attempt to get in touch with us to see how we all were after this terrifying ordeal. The doctor became more aware of the trauma suffered the next day a circular letter was put out to all residents . Obviously all the residents were nervous and anxious at what could happen next and they also needed help. The company put this statement forward :

"Following   the   terrorist   incidents   of Saturday/ Sunday 29/30 may   2004,   The medical centre has been dealing with the most   severely   traumatized   individuals. Understandably,   there   is   still   a   greater number of our people in the community who are suffering and may need help. As ever, we are contactable around the clock for advice and will endeavour to aid you in whatever way we can.

Additionally , The company has arranged for a Critical Incident Debriefer to visit Dharan this weekend. Dr Phillipa Kirkpatrick is a highly qualified and is experienced from last years Riyadh bombings.

Dr Kirkpatrick will hold four group sessions of debriefing. To save travelling time these will be held on each of the four MFS compounds, it is open to all. These are not described as counselling sessions and may even be uncomfortable for those attending. The aim is to reduce the likelihood of post-traumatic stress developing. If you wish to attend please contact the medical centre. We will assess each request and prioritise on the basis of need".

Early evening my dear friend Angie knocked the patio doors to the villa. Angie was one of my dearest friends Dave , Ben, Aimee and I had grown to love her like a a family member she was a blessing to have on the compound always jolly and would talk to everyone a true friend. "Hi Love" Angie said , and put her arms around me, we both started to cry. "Listen Dawn I know you probably don't feel like it but would you be able to come to the social facility with me for a short while , all the girls are there, they wanted to see you yesterday but we understand that you obviously wanted your space after all you have been through. "Oh I don't know Angie I don't like to go outside I still feel a bit nervous" Come on I am not taking no for an answer Angie replied. I sensed Angie was up to something she was not normally this pushy, David, Ben and I followed Angie down the street . I was so frightened of being outside I wasn't ready for the outside world I just wanted to go back indoors. We arrived at the social facility and I opened the door, to my surprise I looked around everyone was cheering! What was this, what was going on? What a wonderful surprise I could hardly take it all in. My eyes filled up, I looked up, On every wall there were picture frames with sweet little quotes, one of them read " what is a mother " Beautiful baby verses dotted around the room. There was a small wooden clown a little toy for Jacob for when he arrived! A beautiful blue and yellow moses basket with a matching baby quilt with padded sheep. A baby bouncer, teddy bears and lots more. I walked around the room with tears in my eyes and thanked everyone for their generosity and kindness , I was choked to be honest at how wonderful, and how thoughtful everyone had been. I spent a while going around the room thanking everyone and in turn my friends were saying how sorry and worried they had been when they had heard about us being trapped in the compound .The sad thing was they had decorated the facility with balloons and ribbons the day before the attack they were trying to keep it all a secret about the baby shower they had all had a part of arranging. Everyone told us that when we were inside the Oasis compound they were praying that we would all make it out alive.

After a while we headed back to our villa, exhausted and overwhelmed by the kindness of my many friends. I was so thankful to be alive, every minute counted every breath I was grateful for but still the flashbacks were too hard for me to cope with I was truly exhausted. Was I ever going to be able to have a normal life ever again? I was so jumpy nervous a single estranged noise would make me shiver . I spent the rest of the day calling my family back home and writing emails just to reassure them that I was okay. My dad who was presently living in Thailand wrote to me,

"Hi Dawn, I am so glad that you are safe and well, I know it must be shocking to see dead people everywhere and you have seen terrible things that grown men couldn't even handle, but you have to move on and build your strength on the fact that you have survived this massive ordeal.

I saw a lot of dead people in the second world war and I know these things can stay with you for a very long time. Remember the monk you came to see in Thailand when you came to visit ? His words were that this baby shall bring you luck, well I think that was proven yesterday , your time wasn't up. I tried your mobile number in Saudi yesterday lots but I couldn't get through. Promise me now that you won't leave the compound and stay safe indoors. These terrorists are animals and should be treated as such. Take Care Dawn, keep in touch, I love you Dad" xxx

My dad always brought comfort with his kind words and I know he must have been very frightened but everyone could relax now nothing was going to happen to me, I was safely home with my unborn child and family I couldn't be happier. The next few months proved very hard for all of us.

On the 31st May one of our friends who was a doctor employed by the company wrote a very caring letter, we were very grateful for his concern and words regarding the incident , he was very concerned for the welfare of all who were involved .

The Doctor wrote:
Management Meeting 31st May 2004:

Following the security incident on Saturday and the meeting with the Ambassador yesterday, I would like to make some observations which I would be grateful if you could feed into the management meeting this afternoon.

The ladies from Las Dunas who were on the bus to Oasis on Saturday morning and subsequently trapped there for the rest of the day were palpably angry yesterday about what they saw as the Company's lack of interest in them after the incident and that no-one was forthcoming to debrief them. I understand that Dr A. eventually came to see them but only after being requested to do so by David Hornsey, Dawns husband. It seems that Dr A. had been informed that they were alright and that there was no need for any follow up.If it was the case that the Company believed that these ladies were fine and did not need any debriefing then I have to say that this was naïve, it should have obvious that they were likely to have been severely traumatised and at the very least someone from the Company should have gone to see them yesterday to see how they were doing. I appreciate that people are busy at a time like this but what about improvising? As an executive grade living on Las Dunas I would of been happy to help with this sort of thing (I do after all have some experience of it, that's why I am writing this), I only needed to be briefed and asked. However, the ladies concerned have informed me and my wife this morning that someone from the Company coming to see them in an official capacity would have been helpful. As it is I have been informed that the Las Dunas ladies are still in a bad way and that at least one of the ladies is still very angry about what she sees as the Company's indifference. One other point that I have been asked to pass on is that the husband of one of the ladies asked his supervisor on Saturday for the following day off to comfort his wife, he was told not to forget to do it officially. This has to be insensitive management at its worst and was particularly galling for him when he sees the seniors in his department being given frequent time off for family members and and the like.

The Amabassador's meeting yesterday was welcome if for no other reason that this was the first time in my five years here that I have been aware of the embassy making a visible effort on our behalf. Some points arising out of this:

The Amabassador said that there was no intelligence indicating that this incident was in the offing . However last week I noticed two unusual things. On Thursday morning while shopping in Al Khobar I remarked to my wife how quiet the roads were . I was able to cross the Corniche road outside the Gulf Centre while the lights were green without waiting, not once but twice. Perhaps it was just because it was the end of the month but I have never seen a Thursday morning outside of Ramadan with so little traffic. Moreover last Wednesday morning the mosque near the airbase hospital was delivering a very loud Ramadan Type harangue. Then yesterday a teacher from TSI told me how last week he had noticed an airbase mosque also delivering a loud and angry address. Taken by themselves these may seem to be of little significance, However if there was a route by which information like this could be cascaded upwards, a bigger picture might emerge. It may be no more than a possible change In the atmosphere about town but that sort of information could be passed down so that the people can make their own decisions on venturing out. The Security notices as they are lose their impact because they always say the same thing. It is all very well for us to complain that there is no intelligence but we could all do our bit to feed information in.

Lastly, a practical point. I am sure we all appreciate the the Metropolitan Police officers have come here at short notice to assist with the investigation. The Amabassador asked anyone who may be able to help them to come forward and so my wife alerted them to our neighbours on Las Dunas. The Officers gave us their mobile phone numbers, all of which began 0044.

Surely it is not without the wit of man to provide them with local phone numbers while they are here.

Signed Dr .B

The next day David went back to work and my feelings were of mixed anxiety. The slightest sound outside made me shiver. I was so nervous that a similar incident would happen again. I picked the phone up and called David's work number, I got through to his workshop. "Hello" David supervisor answered. "Hi Is David there please I need to talk with him please" He told me that David was in a meeting and that not to worry he would send the message straight away. I thanked him and waited for the phone to ring. David was in another office arranging time off , sorting out all our tickets to fly home that very evening. David didn't have much time off but was trying to negotiate more time as needed to save it for the birth of our child. Richard David's work colleague had received the forwarding message from the supervisor that I had called. Richard had worked in the kingdom a considerably number of years and was well liked by many people he was a kind easy going kind of guy and very loyal. Richard had a quick word with David and told him not to worry that he would come and visit me . Richard knocked the villa door and I was so relieved to see him. I made him a cup of tea and we sat and talked and talked about family and Richard told me that it was ok and normal to be feeling the way I was feeling and that in the future things will get easier. Richard told me that everything was nearly sorted and David would be home soon and was just waiting on the tickets being printed out and that he had sorted out the leave . As soon as David returned home from work I felt safe again and knew it would be just a few more hours before we would be heading home to our family . A few of my friends came to say goodbye again and hoped that we would be able to make it back and that they would look forward to seeing the new baby .

The taxi pulled up at the villa, I looked back and wondered if I would ever be able to come back here to the place that had been my home , leaving my friends was hard to do but I had to be safe again and leave it was my time to go. I climbed into the taxi and crawled onto the floor behind the driver's seat. I would be safe here I thought nobody would see me, I was so scared , David said nothing and supported me in anything I was doing as he knew it could just take that one moment where I could lose it . It seemed forever travelling to Bahrain but it was one step closer to getting back home to Britain.

Finally after the long drive from Dhahran to Bahrain we were here. The worst part of this Journey was going through Customs on the causeway which is between Dhahran in Saudi Arabia and Bahrain. The sound of the car engines were deafening "beep" "beep" shouting, shaking of the fists were all a thing we had been accustomed to. It was worth the wait it usually took about forty five minutes on a good day but could several hours with a tailback of traffic. Once you were past customs and into Bahrain you had a sense of freedom. There were still Saudi laws that had to be followed but generally there was a relaxed aura about the place. A lot of the expat community would take long weekends and meet up with each other and stay in the many luxurious hotels serving alcohol and fine foods. One of our favourite restaurants in Bahrain was a lovely Mexican restaurant hidden away in a side street. The owner of the restaurant was of African origin and would always wear a bright dazzling white suit with a very large white smile to match!

After having our meal we would usually move on to one of the many shopping malls in Bahrain. One of our favourites was the Seef Mall.

We were finally here our departure was merely a few hours away. David , Ben and I talked about all the good times that we had had here in the kingdom and it was a good cultural experience for all of us but it was our time to go now.

We started to descend down the runway. Any minute now we would take off and we would return home onto British soil. We started to taxi down the runway, I stared out of the window until Saudi looked like a dot in the distance . Would we ever come back ?. My thoughts were with all my family now and the sheer excitement of seeing them all . I spent the next few hours of the flight thinking about what it would be like seeing my mother , Father and Aimee again . I drifted off to sleep with these lovely thoughts in my mind.

I was awoken by Ben touching my arm. "Mum we are about to land, look mum its London, It feels so glad to be back in Britain". "Let's not look back in anger let's look forward to the future" Ben had always had a lovely way with words . I Looked up and could see the airport out of the window. Yes we were here !

Earlier in the week we had been prewarned that on entering the airport we would be hurried through incase of the press, reporters etc. We would be met by the duty manager and taken through a different route to avoid the media.

We had received a phone call in Saudi from David's Uncle Richard who worked for the BBC as a News engineer.

We gathered our hand luggage together and headed our way towards the exit doors. The air was cold and crisp and very refreshing after the long flight home. We headed towards the first arrival gate, we were not met by anyone, we were still unsure what was going to happen we carried on towards arrivals. There was the usual chaos and people greeting each other. There were tears and smiles. Have you ever stopped and looked closely at people's faces emotions in an airport it can be a very happy but also a very sad place to be, people saying their goodbyes to loved ones, maybe they had several months before they would meet again. There were people over excited, maybe it was their brother their cousin boyfriend etc. Everyone here had a story to tell. Luckily we got through to the main exit doors with no press. The news had obviously died down about the events of May 29th in Britain. Obviously in Saudi it had had a larger Tv/Media coverage. I felt for my friends I had left behind and hoped and prayed they would stay safe. A lot of my friends were planning on taking longer breaks home this time and to decide if they were going to return to Saudi or not.

We headed out of the airport towards the hire car offices. David sorted out the paperwork for the hire car as soon as we had packed the car we were on our way to Wales. Finally after a few stops for coffee breaks etc we were home. It felt strange being home again, It was lovely to be back again in my own safe surroundings .

The next few days were taken up sorting and arranging the house. Aimee came to visit it, it was so lovely to hold her again and we talked and talked about our unborn babies and how strange and funny it was that we were pregnant together and how Jacob would be an Uncle to her baby and exciting that I would be a a grandmother. We shopped for baby clothes and David and I bought Aimee her first pushchair Mamas and Papas, they were quite expensive but very sturdy.

June would prove a busy month , we had to look around for the best suitable boarding school for Ben. We didn't want Ben to go back to Saudi as we felt it would be too risky travelling by bus across the Khobar to the school. The International school was a very good school and well guarded but also clearly a prime target of interest for any terrorist groups. If I were to go back at least I would not have to worry that Ben would not be in any danger. Women could not drive in Saudi so we had to rely on buses or the majority of time the women used taxis which was a challenge in itself with the bustling and heaving traffic.

Hours and hours were spent trawling the internet sending emails making shortlists etc. Finally narrowing down to a possible three private schools we arranged to visit two out of the three of them. One was in Yorkshire, and the other in Cumbria. Ben loved the great outdoors and maybe in his free-time he could venture out and do some rock climbing , and hiking. Life would change for the better for him as living in Saudi we were protected living on a compound and unless you ventured out into the desert there was not that much else to do. David and I discussed and studied Bens options and the advantages and disadvantages of both schools , David decided that I should stay at home whilst they both looked at the schools , as the travelling was a bit much and I could spend a lot more time with Aimee. David was right I would just hold them back being a bit slower. Ben decided that he preferred the school in Cumbria and it was more suitable for him. The school was a mix of both, a state school for local students non boarders, it had a boarding section for international students from as far as Japan! It offered a wide range of sports facilities and with outdoor activities. The scenery around the Lake District was absolutely beautiful. Ben was very excited for his new adventure but at the same time apprehensive which was understandable. Leaving the family would be hard, we received a letter from his selected school of choice, Ben would start his first term in the September.

Chapter 6

I had received an email for an appointment with Dr Fitzgerald to be debriefed. It read :

As discussed Dr Philippa Lewis will conduct a Critical Incident Debriefing session for you, on Friday 11th June at 1300hrs. The meeting would take place at the Hilton Hotel Cardiff. I discussed the matter with David, we both decided maybe it would be a good idea to attend the debriefing as it would help me bring a little closure. I didn't know what to expect, I was a little apprehensive about all . I was still in touch with Erica and she also had decided to accept her appointment .

The day had come we were on our way to Cardiff for the debriefing. David wanted to come along to support me which was comforting. As we approached the Hotel entrance Erica walked outside looking a little tired but relieved she had gone through with it . "How did it go Erica?" Was it okay the meeting?" "Yes Dawn it went well and I am glad I came." Good luck with yours and let me know how it goes". Erica put her arms around me and said Goodbye. We gave our name at the reception desk and the lady told us to go to the 3rd floor and gave me the room number. I knocked quietly on the door a little nervous at what to expect. Dr Fitzgerald answered the door. A kind looking lady with medium length blonde hair opened the door, she was in her early 50s.

" Hello you must be Dawn". "Yes" I replied, and shook her hand. Before we got any further Dr Fitzgerald asked who I was with. I told her it was my husband David and that I would like him to join me as I felt a little unsettled about the whole meeting. She pointed out that she would rather David stayed outside as it was important to have no interruptions during the debriefing . A wave of anxiety came over me and didn't think I could go through with the meeting without David by my side, he had been my rock through all of this and I needed him here with me. I insisted that he joined me otherwise I could not go through with it. She kindly agreed as long as David would promise he would not say a word . Later I understood why she had said this, I sat down in the chair and looked around the room I felt relaxed and at peace here. "Dawn can you start from the beginning and tell me what it was like for you that day, the way you felt ,the events of the day and finally reaching safety." I started giving my account of the day and it did get very emotional as I was pouring the story out to her. Dr Fitzgerald told me to take it slow and I was doing great. We got to the part where we had all reached the area in the kitchen where we all gathered together and started to line-up and how we had to follow instructions from the soldier who was heading our way out to safety. "Can I stop you there Dawn." "What happened in the kitchen Dawn?" I didn't understand what did she mean? Again she questioned me. "Dawn did

137

anyone join you In the kitchen?" No I couldn't recall anything . I started feeling very confused and worried. Had I left anything out so important that she felt necessary to question me? Finally Dr Fitzgerald told me why she was questioning me." "Dawn when you was in the kitchen Heidi , Mackenzie and Fin came out from behind the refrigerator's didn't they?". I replied "Yes". Why had I forgotten such an important part? How did she know? "How I know Dawn is that I have debriefed others and have heard also that they joined you in the kitchen. " I couldn't believe I could let something slip from my mind that was so very important . "Dawn the reason you blocked them out off your mind is that you are protecting them." "Our minds can play tricks on us sometimes, especially in this case." "You were trying to protect them , that's why your mind chose not to remember when asked." I managed to finish my story giving the correct version of events. I felt relieved with the debriefing. I couldn't help but wonder why David's employers had wanted me to have this debriefing? Was it because they were worried I was going to go public with it all?. I was very suspicious. The company was always struggling to recruit people as Saudi Arabia was becoming an unstable region and theses recent events would not do the recruitment side any favours. To be honest I was wary of everyone right now. The terrorist attack had affected me mentally I do admit but not so much that I was going to crumble and let the terrorists win I was stronger than that , I am stronger than that. I wasn't sure how this meeting was going to help me but somehow I felt better already to talk about what had gone on that day . I shook Dr Fitzgerald's hand and was happy that I had the opportunity to have been debriefed.

We were all very excited today David's parents were coming to stay with us for a few days. They had desperately wanted to see us but understood we needed a few days to settle back in to the normality of things and recover. The last time we had spoken with them was that dreadful day and we all really needed to see each other .

We had half-finished projects over the house and Jeff had offered to come and help us he was very good when it came to decorating and odd jobs . We had the kitchen floor to recement and level , the bathroom to repaper, painting and some electrical work. We had some very sad and worrying news also that Jeff had been diagnosed with prostate cancer and had opted to have surgery. The surgery was not for a few weeks so by coming down and helping out it would pass the time away and take his mind away from worrying too much. Jeff had researched the best possible doctors and was satisfied with the surgeon who was to perform the operation. We were all worried but didn't show it too much as we all had to stay strong and positive. The nearing birth of Jacob had offered Jeff hope and something positive to focus on. Sue and Jeff pulled up in the car outside, we were so excited! Sue was the first one to enter the house we greeted each other and hugged and hugged. "Oh Dawn it's so good to see you my love you poor thing, you had us all worried there for a moment . We were in touch with David throughout it all so we know a little at what had gone on!" Jeff entered the house, David greeted and hugged his Dad you could feel the emotion between them , it felt so good to have mum and dad with us in our home. Jeff looked at me and said "Hello brave young lady , it is really good to see you Dawn." How are you Dawn besides everything?" "I am really well thank you Jeff and better for seeing you both" . How many babies have you in there Dawn? You are pretty big now, it's not long before our Grandchild is born, Sue and I are so excited. After having refreshments and a bite to eat we all exchanged our news. We told

Jeff that we really hoped everything would work out okay and that if he wasn't up to helping us out with our numerous jobs around the house we wouldn't mind and would eventually get them sorted later on as we didn't want to tire him out. He wasn't really supposed to drive long distances due to the medication he was on but nothing was going to stop the both of them from seeing us. Sue explained that her worst fears had come to light the day of the attack, and that she really hoped someday that we could consider moving back home to the uk as she was afraid something like this could happen again in the near future. We didn't mention that we had already decided to go back that would worry them both so much . We thought this wasn't the right time to say . They had so much to worry about themselves yet they were here today helping us out they were so kind and unselfish. The next day Ben and David mixed the self-levelling compound and Jeff and David poured it on the floor. It was the first time any of them had tried it . It was looking good and there was a lot of pleased faces in the house that day. It was really nice to see the house improving very rewarding for all of us . The next job was fitting all the doors on downstairs. David had removed them a few years previously . The reason was was that our daughter Aimee had had an argument with her father as children do and she had run downstairs like a bolt of lightning and tripped up on some ironing in the hallway and fell directly into a glass door . It was horrific ! Luckily she had a very small cut to her forehead just above her eyebrow any nearer and she could of lost her eye. The poor child had to have 4 stitches . After this accident David had insisted that the doors were to be removed in our house and would be replaced with wooden ones.

David started to make calls back to work already arranging his trip back to Saudi. I didn't want him to leave us . I was frightened for him, especially being seven months pregnant now and so close to the birth. Saudi Arabia was a long way away if I was to go into Labour.

Once David had returned back in the kingdom Of Saudi Arabia had arranged his tickets for his flight black several times , not wishing to break in on any holiday entitlement which he had saved for the birth.

David had become embroiled in discussions with the company arranging his time off. Ultimately they generously offered 6 weeks of reduced pay, plus allowed him to owe up to 3 weeks holiday. I was so glad David had been able to spend time with me when we returned back to the uk from Saudi as it was a very hard time, I knew I would handle matters better with David by my side. David was apprehensive in leaving me but I assured him I had lots of friends and family and that I was moving on now and that everything would be okay .

David settled back in to work over the next few days. The manpower had been seriously hindered, with the large number of people that had left and also who were about to leave after given three months notice. Obviously the terrorist attack had had a large impact on people's minds and their families wanted them home . People were just genuinely frightened. The day after the attack around 168 people had put their notice in, over ten percent of the workforce were leaving.

We enjoyed our evenings telephoning each other and catching up on news about the children, hospital appointments, and what generally people were saying back in Saudi about the the incident.. David told me that he was the sole advisor now in his workshop everyone had left and that they were trying to recruit people but there was not much interest which was understandable.

I discussed with David that the best way forward for us financially and for the future would be to return to Saudi Arabia once Jacob had been born and maybe I could join David when Jacob was around 3 months old as he would need his checks and injections first.

Everything was going to plan and David was kept very busy after work sorting the house out as five weeks would just fly by now before coming back home again. It was nice to see David so looking forward to us being together again.

A previously owned 4x4 Galloper was purchased with air conditioning a large car than we previously had and for the safety side of things.. I enjoyed my conversations with David telling me that he had nearly finished building the cot for Jacob and that he had placed it inbetween the two walls opposite the door. The door to our bedroom was a 300kg blast door which had been fitted to all the villas on the compound as part of the safety programme. Also the windows had anti shatter film placed over them incase of a bomb blast the glass would stay on the sheeting causing less damage. On the other side of the room . David had stocked up on emergency supplies already nappies , spare clothes, creams and later on would provide dried milk and nibbles for Jacob incase of another lockdown incident. With not being able to get off the compound it would become a sanctuary. We had to think ahead as a family .

The Homecoming , 6 weeks had passed so quickly. We were all so excited David was coming home today. I felt so secure knowing that he would make it for the birth. I can't tell you how happy I was. I spent most of the day preparing the meal for the evening . David always enjoyed my cooking, I enjoyed cooking for him too .

David picked up the hire car up at the airport and gave me a call "Dawn I am here thank heavens I can be here for you now you don't know how much a relief it is for me". "I do know love" I replied, "I have felt the same way about your homecoming, please drive carefully and I will see you in a few hours." I decided to take a nap that would pass the hours away for sure and in no time David would be home.

I was awoken with a warm familiar hand stroking my forehead.
I looked up and was so happy to have my husband back home again. We hugged each other for a while and talked about how I was and how Aimee was also coping with her pregnancy. There wasn't much room on the settee for the two of us anymore I must have had the biggest baby bump ever! David told me that everyone had sent their regards from Saudi and to wish us all the best of luck for

the birth. My life was perfect right now he was home.

Chapter 7

So here I am in the labour room waiting to meet my little soldier... It has been a long journey waiting for this very special moment, I cannot tell you how emotional this first meeting was going to be, as we nearly didn't make it .   My thoughts, I thought back, I survived ......We survived ....The fear, the anxiety , the unknown . That day will never leave me as long as I shall live.

The birth of this child was new hope a new beginning . We were so excited to meet our child. He was rather special already . I looked all around at the labour room it was quite and homely compared to the other rooms I had had the experience of giving birth in. There was a tiny poster on the wall opposite me of a newly born baby smiling lying on his mother's breast, I couldn't help but to smile back. David was by my side as he always was with a look of worry and excitement. I had a good feeling about this birth, I was so excited myself. "Dawn dear it won't be long now" said the midwife. A heavy feeling came all over me and the urge to push was so immense , could this be it? Yes it was! In my head all I could do was stay focused and help this little man begin his journey into this world . My body had now entered another dimension, I slipped away into the pain and tried to focus on the positive result at the end of it . The midwife told me that little Jacob had fallen asleep and that I wouldn't be allowed any pain relief as it would slow the birth down. Okay Jacob wake up darling you are going to meet your mummy and daddy . I looked up and stared into my husband's beautiful blue eyes to help me through the pain , I kept repeating out loud "beautiful blue eyes, beautiful blue eyes"! David gripped my hand tightly and whispered in my ear you can do it Dawn come on darling I love you .

Pushing lasted an eternity I slowly came back to reality.. I was so exhausted it took all the strength I had to look up . Jacob was here! My child had been born! I had done it we had done it! Finally it was all over, our beautiful little boy was here with us. "Oh Dawn he is a big one" shouted the Midwife. I looked up and couldn't believe my eyes he had the biggest cheeks you had ever seen and was looking straight at me , he looked like a little Eskimo all blue, big eyes and those fantastic big cheeks ."Oh my look at his cheeks"! I rejoiced! The midwife passed him over to me but I couldn't lift my hands up to hold him . Jacob Was nine pounds born and a whopper! I was so weak so exhausted but so happy. I asked David to hold him and I was so glad to see the two of them together, David was so overwhelmed. A few hours later I woke up in the post-natal ward, it was rather noisy here to be expected. Jacob lay asleep in the little plastic cot by the side of me. I continued for the next hour just staring at him checking every little detail his toes his fingers and hair. I picked him up and the warmth and smell of my new baby was so comforting. "Hello little man I whispered in his ear", your safe now Jacob. Jacob settled down between the large v cushion David had brought me , it was such a shame to move him now and there was hardly any room in the plastic cot the hospital had given me , it was Jacobs cheeks they had seem to double in size in just a few hours! Mr Cheeks slept through the night on my bed like a little puppy .

The next day I was moved to a quiet little room on my own with Jacob, it was a pleasant little room and a lot quieter I was thankful of the peace. In the corner there was a large fish tank it was relaxing to watch and would often send me off to sleep.

A few hours later Aimee entered the room and was smiling from cheek to cheek too. Aimee picked Jacob up in her arms and had tears in her eyes. Aimee only had one or two weeks left to go until the birth of her first child herself. All the excitement was overwhelming. I was a mother again for the third time and I was going to be a grandmother in less than a fortnight! I felt very lucky and fortunate to have all of this. "Oh Mum he is absolutely beautiful , he looks like a little Eskimo baby he is so big mum , how are you feeling are you okay?" "Yes my darling I am great thank you, and how are you?"

"I feel so excited now mum after seeing Jacob to know I will have a baby very soon too". We talked and talked and I thought how wonderful and lucky I was to have three beautiful children, a wonderful gift. Later that day mum and my stepdad came to visit also .

Everyone was eager to see the new addition to the family. Mums knees were hurting her she had suffered a few years with this and dad had bought her a wheelchair to help her out and about. Dad wheeled mum in and they both stopped by the side of Jacobs tiny plastic cot and couldn't help but look at him. I looked up and they both had tears in their eyes also . I think all who saw Jacob felt that it was a very special moment and were so glad he was finally here. I got out of my bed and asked mum would she like to hold him ? "Yes Dawn , I would love to". From that moment on until this day my mother has a very special bond with Jacob, he has given her a very special will to hold on to things dear in her life and most of all he gives her hope.

Jacob and I had all our checks and later that afternoon we were fit to go home to start our new life together.

It felt good being home again. I could relax and look after Jacob better at home, I had everything I needed here. David was a great help over the next few days and he was running around doing all the chores while I looked after Jacob. I had decided to breastfeed Jacob as I had never attempted it on my other children but knew this would be the last chance I had so I had decided to go ahead with it. After a few days Jacob started to look pale and very weak but seemed to be fine. We had a hospital check today I was getting rather concerned as he was not improving at all and just knew something wasn't quite right. I didn't want to sound like an overconcerned new mother afterall this was my third child. We waited in the corridor anxiously and finally it was our turn to see the doctor. Jacob was weighed and the baby nurse looked over to me a bit shocked. She weighed Jacob again….Dawn Jacob has lost over twenty five percent of his bodyweight, we are going to have to admit you both as he is getting severely dehydrated darling". "Don't worry this sometimes happens when you are new to breastfeeding." Jacob wasn't getting sufficient milk I felt so guilty and started to feel very concerned. The doctor came to see us and explained it maybe better to half breastfeed him and half bottle feed him so that way they could check to see how much milk he was intaking. As I lay on the hospital bed I couldn't help but cry I had nearly killed my baby starving him to death! Jacob was very poorly now and all I could think of was getting some fluids into him. Jacob was so dehydrated he didn't seemed bothered to take it. Sip by sip he started to drink . Jacob was just six pounds and a few ounces , a big drop in the nine pounds he was being born. I thought about giving up with the breastfeeding but that would be giving in too easy. It was something that we would have to tackle together. After a few days in hospital we were allowed home again, Jacob had finally satisfied the nurses and his weight thankfully was now increasing. Breastfeeding was overtaking the bottle, I was so pleased that I hadn't given in. Jacob seemed more settled with his surroundings at home now too. We were all getting excited for the arrival of my daughter's baby any day now. The time was nearing and I could see that she was getting more and more tired. How our lives would change again over the next few weeks. It had been an emotional few months but we as a family seemed to tackle everything as it happened we always did we were strong family unit.

It was mid afternoon.........
We had received the call we had been waiting for! David came running into the living room "Dawn, Dawn Aimee is in labour!" My heart was rushing and felt very heavy, all I could think about was Aimee going through all the pains of labour I don't think I could bear her

suffering , it was a pain that would change her life and she would have a precious reward after it . My heart was telling me to go to her. I so wanted to be there for her but I couldn't leave Jacob now as I was breastfeeding him regularly and we had finally worked out what we were both doing! David turned to me and said "Dawn I know as her mother you feel like running to her right now but I can be there for her for both of us. You know how much I love her and I have always been the one to calm her, let me do it it would be an honour. "Aimee's partner had never been very supportive in the past so we both knew that one of us had to be there for her. I agreed , David told me he would call me as often as he could and not to worry that he would take good care of her. As the door closed behind him I couldn't help but feel useless and just wanted to run to my daughter to be with her. I was being silly and not thinking straight I would only get in the way and it wouldn't be fair to Jacob. I called my mum and Sue my mother in law to tell them the news. Everyone was so excited and overwhelmed that there would be another new addition to the family very soon. They were all very lucky, I promised I would keep everyone updated.

David arrived within half an hour of Aimee's call. Aimee appeared fairly comfortable but obviously looked very anxious this being her first child. She was so glad to have her father by her side. The two of them were so close and David knew how to cheer her up even with his bad jokes!

As the hours moved on her pain and discomfort increased. David called me, "Everything is okay, I don't think it's going to be too long Dawn now, don't worry she is doing fine." I told David to tell Aimee that I loved her dearly and that I would come to see her as soon as I could .The Anaesthetist had been called as Aimee had been offered pethidine or an epidural , she had opted for an epidural. Aimee had to wait a further forty minutes as the anaesthetist was busy in theatre. She started to feel and look more anxious as the pain grew stronger. David held her hand and told her she was doing very well. David tried to hide his emotions. It was very hard to see your child in pain and suffering but knew they were would be happiness and a birth of his grandchild when it was all over. It wasn't easy watching your loved one like this.

Aimee was getting more and more anxious now "Dad when am I going to have my epidural? I need it now! Dad I don't think I can do it, it's the pain I can't take anymore, am I going to die?" David picked up her other hand and put her two hands together in his. "Look at me , look into my eyes" David looked deep into his daughters eyes, as she did his." You are not going to die , I am here and I am going to stay here to look after you I am always here for you, you will be fine honestly, I will not let anything happen to you'. Aimee smiled it spoke volumes. David knew he couldn't remove her pain but could reassure her by just being there. Their faith in each other helped Aimee and her father get through the night. Finally the anaesthetist entered the room. Aimee looked up and commented to her father how handsome the anaesthetist looked , David found it highly amusing that Aimee could think this whilst being in pain. The anaesthetist reassured Aimee that she would have her epidural soon. As soon as it was administered Aimee felt calm and was finally feeling some relief. The nurses were changing shifts and one of them recognised David. "Have I seen you somewhere else before one of the nurses asked?" "Yes I was here a fortnight ago with my wife for the birth of our son Jacob." David had spent a good part of the last fortnight in the maternity wing and post-natal ward visiting Jacob and I. He told the nurse that he understood how to operate the monitor if they needed an extra pair of hands. After a thought or two the nurses allowed David to help out with the monitor while they concentrated on helping Aimee.

David took an opportunity for a break and walked into the corridor and called to update me with the news.

Another hour passed and the signs of the baby being born was imminent. Eventually that amazing moment had arrived when our beautiful grandson was born. David and his baby grandsons eyes met, it was another moment he would never forget. He looked up at Aimee and had tears in his eyes. "Aimee it's a boy, it's a boy! Look Aimee look what you have, a beautiful baby isn't it just wonderful a moment we shall always treasure together, I told you I wouldn't let anything happen to you. I am so proud today to be your father! I had better call your mum she will be so pleased to know you are both doing fine, now try and rest and enjoy your cuddles with your little boy. Aimee was so delighted and thankful it was all over. "Dad thank you for staying with me throughout it all I couldn't have done it without you , I love you dad".

I had been overwhelmed with worry as I hadn't heard from David in a little while and my motherly instinct was telling me the birth was near I just needed to know that everything was okay.

David called me with the delightful news. "Dawn it's all over you will be so pleased to know we have a grandson he is so beautiful and Aimee is doing great she is obviously very tired but is resting now. I am exhausted but so proud of our daughter today.

An hour or so later David arrived home so tired but so happy." "I will take you in the morning to see Aimee and the baby Dawn they are both sleeping now". I think I could sleep for a week after all that." "What a wonderful day it has been".

The next morning I couldn't wait to leave for the hospital. David seemed well after a good night's sleep but surely could of done with a few hours more. We pulled up into the hospital grounds. I couldn't wait to see them both, I hurried my way in through the hospital corridors not blinded by anyone in my path. Finally, I entered the room and looked over to them both. I looked over towards the cot I couldn't believe my beautiful daughter was a mother now. She looked so happy and contented , it suited her being a mother she was constantly staring at her baby checking him over." "Aimee my darling I am so glad your both okay, I am sorry I wasn't with you my love but I think Dad did a pretty good job ". I held Aimee for a long time. I looked over to the little cot besides the bed and turned to my daughter. "Aimee have you named him yet?" "Yes mum I have, I have called him Morgan".

"Hello Morgan beautiful, I am your grandmother," he was all snuggled up in his little blanket. There was a huge feeling of love in the room, my eyes filled up, I walked over to the little plastic cot and slowly reached in to pick him up. It was pure joy holding my grandson for the first time, a moment any grandparent can tell you indescribable. We were so fortunate to have two healthy babies born into the family within two weeks of each other. I held Jacob over the cot and introduced them both. , "Jacob this is your nephew Morgan, Morgan this is your uncle". We all giggled at the fact there was only two weeks between them and how funny it all seemed.

Over the next few weeks David had the opportunity to bond with Jacob and was of course the doting dad and grandad. It was lovely to see father and son together treasured memories.
David had to return to work fairly soon now after the birth as he had used up a lot of his holiday entitlement and wanted to be home for the Babies for their first Christmas.

This time David would be away for two months, I think it would of been far harder for him than it would myself as I would have my daughter Aimee for company and my grandson . I was such a lucky lady and a very proud mum too. David reluctantly returned to Saudi.

Chapter 8

Two months had flown by and I couldn't wait for David to see Jacob again . I think he would be very shocked how much he had grown and developed. Jacob had more hair and was smiling and trying to move slightly on his side. To be honest I had thought a lot while David was away and I how I hated the separation, in the long term it would be better for us to be all together. I was missing my Saudi friends also, and things had quietened down now in Saudi, there was tightened security implemented everywhere.

David was home once again. David said that it was an amazing feeling to be able to touch Jacob again, he had even missed the babies crying!

The family gathered around for Christmas. This was such a luxury to be home for Christmas, usually David was given the choice of every other year due to the lack of manpower in his workshop but was fortunate to have cover for this Christmas. Christmas was not celebrated in Saudi Arabia but they did have Christmas trees decorated in the shopping malls in Bahrain. We would try and visit a week before Christmas just to be able to see the decorated malls. We were all so happy this year and blessed to have all our family so near and dear to us on British soil. You really appreciate your time at home the smells of Cinnamon candles, the mince pies and not to forget the Christmas carols. Jacob and Morgan were too young to understand what was going on although they did enjoy the Christmas lights for a few hours.

David had planned to return to Saudi before the New Year . I didn't mind too much as I was busy with Jacob and still enjoying my little grandson and my time with Aimee and Ben. I knew this would be the last time David would return on his own. Over the Christmas period David had received numerous amount of emails which he didn't want me to know about.

The Wardens notice would read:

There has been calls for demonstrations in Saudi Arabia on Thursday 16th December. We do not know when or where any such demonstration might take place.

We therefore re-iterate our long standing advice to avoid public gatherings.

The Foreign and Commonwealth office revised their Travel Advice for Saudi Arabia. Earlier in the year in October there had been an incident outside the Seder Village Compound in Riyadh. Several shots had been fired targeted towards the compound, the terrorists had entered and killed two Pakistani women , one was believed to have been pregnant.

The Foreign Commonwealth Office released the following statement :

We continue to believe that Terrorists are planning further attacks. People who choose to remain in the kingdom should maintain the highest level of vigilance. They should take all necessary steps to protect their safety and family and to ensure they have confidence in their individual security arrangements.

We would also advise against drawing unnecessary attention to yourself , and to observe modesty in your dress and behaviour.

HM consul

On the 21st of December David received an email from the company HR Manager which was rather shocking and very unexpected. He insisted that David was not to return to Saudi Arabia without a full psychiatric report, stating that he was fit and mentally stable to return to work. If he was to return beforehand he would be disciplined. I was shocked and saddened to think that the company were causing us much grief when we were only trying to step in the right direction and move forward. David called around several Special Psychologists but as you can imagine over the Christmas period they were either starting their holidays or fully booked. Finally we were in luck an appointment was made but it was the same day he was due to fly back. David called the HR Department in Saudi and explained that he had to arrange a private appointment, otherwise he would have to wait over six months for an appointment. Even so the private appointment would take about three weeks to sort out waiting for medical reports etc. The HR manager replied "David We have agreed to pay for the fees for the Psychologists and request that in the meantime you shall provide sicknotes for the time off from work. "David explained that this could not be possible as he was not in his opinion ill. Eventually they accepted David's position.

We tried not to let this negative news get us down and carried on enjoying the festivities the best we could with our family . David also had time to finish off the DIY jobs at home. In a way I was secretly pleased he wasn't going back for a few more weeks. Every week Jacob was developing and it was just nice that David would be here to share these precious moments. The day of the appointment had arrived. David explained that he needed a report on his mental state of Mind/Health to be allowed to return to work. The doctor was surprised and found it quite amusing as he explained that the two thirds of his work involved writing reports for employees to have time off from work. It was the first time he had been asked for a report to allow someone to return to work. In the meantime David was contacted by Human Resources several times asking where the medical report was and when they can expect to receive it. He had already stated previously in his emails that the report would take up to three weeks to process. Human Resources were causing David stress it was starting to annoy him deeply and felt that they were not very understanding regarding all that had happened throughout the year.

The next morning David checked his emails and again HR were being unreasonable. The specialist had advised David that he would write his report and send it Asap i.e in the next few weeks, which was a reasonable time to expect it to be written.

HR's Email read:

Dear Mr Hornsey , I note that you went to see a specialist yesterday (24th January 05), Having just spoken with the medical centre they do not have seemed to have received it yet. Please can you advise as to when they are likely to receive this so that they can determine your fitness to return to KSA.

The sooner this is received the quicker the decision can be made, and if there is likely to be a delay in this being processed, it would be appreciated if you could advise accordingly.

Graham
HR Advisor

David wrote back :

Dear Graham, you can be assured of my desire to return to work at the earliest possible date, in fact I had hoped to return to KSA on the 29th, December 2004. Any delay to my return to the kingdom has been to HR's request for this report. By pressing for a private referral. I have speeded up the process to assure my return at the earliest that is practical taking into account the time of the year and the availability of free appointment slots. I do appreciate The Companies concern with regard to my health, however as previously stated HR have been informed of my well-being by myself on several occasions. It is in everyone's interest that I return to work at the earliest possible date, however I cannot be held accountable for the delay to my return to work, Hopefully I will be allowed to get on with my job on my return unhindered! As soon as I receive the report I shall fax it to the medical centre the same day. I shall notify yourself by email,

Regards David

HR replied :   A   week or two was a little excessive and could David ask the consultant to push it through quicker.

eleven days later the medical report arrived thankfully David could now inform the Company and put an end to all the stresses and strains of trying to return to work, afterall he was only doing as requested . All of this could have been sorted quicker if he had been able to see his family doctor.

On the 7th February , 2005 David received his medical report it read:

I assessed David In my consulting room. David, who works as an avionics engineer with Bae Systems is presently posted in AL Khobar, Saudi Arabia. David informs me that in May 2004 his wife, who was twenty four weeks pregnant, was attacked in the school where she worked in by "Terrorists". The members of the terrorist gang targeted the school staff who in desperation used a school bus as a cover while trying to think of a safe exit onto the grounds. David further tells me that his wife and the other ladies on the bus could hear the crossfire but managed to avoid being shot and escape any major injuries by hiding and lying down on the floor of the bus. She eventually managed to escape from the vehicle and headed towards the building with her colleagues to try and make their way to a safe haven still hearing the crossfire overhead.

Following this terrifying and unexpected incident David returned to the united kingdom along with his wife. Because of his concern for his wife's health David stayed in the united kingdom for seven weeks and returned to work in Saudi Arabia in July 2004. David's wife was expecting their third child in September 2004 but David's company refused his application for leave to return home to be beside his wife when she really needed him more than ever after suffering through her ordeal. This caused quite a lot of anguish and David tried to maintain his mental state of mind throughout to be strong for his wife. David has been feeling a lot of anguish since the negativeness with the company and has become increasingly anxious and stressed. Following a sickness absence for three weeks in September David returned to work again in early October his work pressure has increased enormously due to the current state of lack of manpower. Understandably people have left their employment in Saudi due to any further repercussions of Terrorism. This has further aggravated his general anxiety symptoms In addition David's wife has been experiencing some problems with her visa application in order to return to Saudi Arabia with further added to his misery.

Since early December David has been feeling increasingly anxious and panicky.   He stated that in December he was quite irritable and frequently lost his temper over trivial matters. From 14th to 29th December 2004 David was once again signed off sick from work. In the last few weeks David's condition has improved to a large extent and he is no longer   experiencing   any   significant psychological problems.

There is nothing significant of note in David's Medical history. His mental health prior to 2004 was stable.

David was born and brought up in Luton and recalls having a very loving family and a happy childhood. David started going to school at the age of five years old and left full time education at the age of seventeen with seven GCSEs. He then went to a local college to study electronics and obtained his ONC. David initially joined the Air Force at the age of eighteen as a Radar Technician. It was whilst in the Air force David learned Avionics. David joined Bae six years ago as an Avionics engineer.

As stated earlier he is presently working in Saudi Arabia in the Al Khobar region. David is a hardworking and conscientious individual. Although he finds his job challenging and exciting he finds it a bit hard sometimes because of the lack of trained staff. David was married in 1988. His wife Dawn is thirty seven years old and is now in good health under the circumstances. David has three children, a daughter and two sons.

When I saw David on the 24th January 2005 he was casually dressed and tidy. He did not exhibit any signs of being depressed or anxious. His thinking was clear and rationale and all his cognitive functions were within normal limits.

It is my conclusion my view, that David had suffered from Generalised Anxiety Disorder . David's anxiety disorder mainly arose because of work pressure and the terrible ordeal his wife suffered in the hands of terrorists in May 2004. David's generalised anxiety disorder has improved significantly in the past few weeks and he is now more or less back to his premorbid level of functioning.

In view of the remarkable and spontaneous improvement I do not see any impediment in David returning to work. Although David would remain vulnerable to further episodes of anxiety in the future given any undue stress he should be able to cope with the demands of his work in his present improved state.

Dr A.
Consultant Psychiatrist

David informed HR that He had received the report ,which he has forwarded to the Medical Centre as promised. The psychiatrist had been in touch with the Company as concerned he had not received payment although the invoice had been sent several days ago.

At last David was able to make arrangements for his return flight. As it had taken a few months to sort out I would be able to return to Saudi Arabia also with Jacob, he had had his necessary injections and checks . We had all we needed now the visas nothing was going to stop us, we all needed to return to a sense of normality and settle down as a family and put all this behind us.

Chapter 9

Over the next few weeks Aimee and I spent a lot of time   together. We would compare

182

baby outfits and talk about how well the babies were coming on. Aimee was such a natural at breastfeeding too, far better than I had managed. I just knew she would be a great mother. The time was getting closer to our return to Saudi, I couldn't bring myself to mention it too much to Aimee as I knew we would both get upset easily. We had grown even closer now as mother and daughter .The babies were always together I knew they were very young but they were aware of each other even at this young age. We decided to go on a little shopping trip for some bits and pieces to take back with me. We arrived at the baby store and both the babies needed feeding . The baby store had a comfortable feeding room, so Aimee and I decided to sit in the comfortable armchairs opposite each other and discussed what we would like to buy after we had finished. There was a little boy in the room he must have been around five years of age and was running back and for the room. Suddenly he found an exit door into the shop and opened and ran through it, so much to the shock of Aimee and myself the whole of the store could see in! We had never laughed so much in all our lives .

As I started to pack my suitcase for our return to Saudi I hesitated and thought was I doing the right thing? Part of me was protecting my child from the real possibility of another attack and was I a bad mother on even thinking of taking him back there? I just followed my instincts and imagined us together as a family unit. Jacob was about five and half months old now and was already changing everyday. David would miss out on a lot if we didn't join him. We only had a few weeks holiday a year so months would pass until we would see each other, so yes, this was right for us right now. My mother and stepdad were not happy and David's mum and dad about us leaving which was understandable but understood we all needed to be together . I placed the last few boxes of Jacob's food in my suitcase it was already packed to the limit, I managed to squeeze a few more boxes in. It was quite difficult to buy certain baby foods in Saudi so I was well prepared. Jacob was a fussy eater even at four and half months old! I enjoyed experimenting with new foods and loved to watch his different gestures when new textures and sharp or sweet foods were introduced. I looked back into the room and spotted rabbit. Oh yes rabbit we must not forget him! Rabbit was like a member of the family. We had bought him in a little Mama and Papas shop before Jacob was born and fell in love with him at first sight. He was beige with blue and white pinstripe dungarees and big floppy ears .

Aimee came to say goodbye that evening. I held my grandson for most of the evening and promised my daughter we would call and video conference as it was so good these days, we could still compare and chat about our babies it didn't have to stop. Time would hopefully go quick and we would be home again.

My heart was breaking but I had to be strong she was my child also and I felt as a mother I should stay.

We arrived at departures London. We had a few more minutes before departure. I couldn't bring myself to call my family as I knew I would hear the anxiety in their voices . David and I had made the decision and we had to stick to it .

Once on board we were shown to our seats we were situated in the front of the middle isle and the aircrew had supplied us with a very small travel cot that fitted onto the wall in front of us. I wondered if Jacob would fit into it as he had rather long legs. I placed him inside it was perfect. Jacob slept for most of the journey he was a good baby

The first few days back were spent sorting Jacobs room. David had done a wonderful job building the cot and his little cot, his bumper set was so sweet with furry little quilted sheep on it. At four and half months old he had already acquired a large wardrobe of clothes. He had been given so many presents friends and family had been so kind. As the weather in Saudi was mainly warm sometimes unbearable, I knew I would be lucky to keep Jacob in his vests and lightsuits . February in Saudi was like a British summer. Well a good British Summer.

Caca knocked at the villa door, I was still rather tired from the flight over here and decided to take a short nap. Caca would be the first friend to meet Jacob, she was a very good friend of ours. children . Caca was only out on a short visit for a few weeks to join her husband. She had lived in the kingdom when Gemma her daughter was attending school there, but decided to leave and support her daughter through college. We all loved Caca she was a lovely lady, a character that everyone warmed to. David showed her to the bedroom tiptoeing into the room, Jacob was sleeping. Caca looked inside the cot "Oh Jacob is so handsome David, I can't wait to give him a cuddle when I see him again. I won't disturb him now but he seems so settled in already bless him". The next day I decided to take Jacob out in his pushchair for his first tour of the compound. I was trying to get him used to the climate, it was a good time of year to be here as the heat was bearable and comfortable. I started to feel settled again in my surroundings. Jacob enjoyed his days by the pool, all the ladies of the compound would make such a fuss of him too. Once a week I would have help with my housework and ironing. David had hired two Indian men to help around the house, it was quite normal for the residents of the compound to hire Houseboy's. Brazino would come in once a week and clean and mop the villa. I was very fortunate as it gave me more precious time to spend with Jacob. Hassan would come to iron for me and would never complain if he had an extra bag to do. Our houseboy's would not see their families very often and it could be three years or more before they would have the privilege to do so. Most of the Indian workers had day jobs and by working on the compound cleaning for us it would give them a second income. They all did work very hard and on the weekends you would see several of them washing and polishing the cars. Most of the workers had family and children back home, their flights back to India were so expensive so most of them would take a trip every three years to visit loved ones. This must have been so hard on them missing out on their children's development and trying to keep the bond there as a parent. Once they had finished their time in Saudi Arabia most of them would be rich enough in their own country to start their own businesses , this is why a lot of them saw their time through.

A few months had passed and Jo the Director of the learning centre had got back in touch with me. "Hi Dawn how are you my lovely?" "We have all missed you and we are so glad that You are back, when are we going to meet Jacob"? "He is so special to us". "Did you realise that another lady on the compound has had her baby too, she had a baby girl and has named her "Hope" she felt it was appropriate and feels blessed having her. "Hi Jo I have giving it a great deal of thought and yes I would like to come back to work". I can't promise how I will feel but I will give it a go". "What childminding facilities have you there for Jacob Jo?" I have to have him near me you understand don't you?" Jo told me that the child nannies could take care of Jacob in the crèche, and that she had already looked into it just incase I would said yes, and that there was a space for Jacob. The little creche was in the building opposite the learning centre on the ground floor. It was so sweet and had a good range of toys and learning aids. It had a large space where the children could run around and play. There was one nanny allocated for every three children. I knew a lot of the ladies working there, as previously in my employment at the Oasis compound I would pop back and for when we needed to ask for extra help in the classroom, or we had a parent interested in joining the crèche. Jo and I arranged to meet up in a weeks time just to look around and to see how I felt being back. To be honest I had missed the children's laughter and their funny little ways. Deep down I had already decided to come back. It wasn't Oasis fault they had been targeted with Terrorism. The children and the residents needed normality in their lives again. The Oasis compound had started rebuilding themselves rising up like a phoenix out of the ashes to a stronger more determined and solid community , it was good to see.

A week passed really quickly and David and I discussed my position of going back to work.

We both seemed happy about it and it would give Jacob the opportunity to mix with the children of his own age, also I wouldn't be too far away from him. Our friends and family back home were obviously concerned but we had decided it was right for us. It would be a very large step to take but I had decided to do it.

The time had come, David pulled up in the car outside the Compound. A lot had changed since I had been away. On entering the compound there were two security check posts the first where the guards would ask to see your identity cards, at the next checkpoint there were Alsatian sniffer dogs, I felt comfortable knowing that these new security checks were implemented.

Finally after passing all the security clearance we came to the last set of gates onto the compound. I stepped out the car with Jacob in my arms, David smiled and told us to have a lovely day, as soon as you need to be picked up let me know and I will come straight away for you both. It must hav also leaving us, I headed towards the gates and stopped by the metal door the gates slowly started to slide open. I took a deep breath paused and looked back holding Jacob tightly by the Heel. "I can do this" I whispered. I stepped through the gates, the first steps were the hardest but after entering the compound I had finally faced my demons, they hadn't won I was stronger now I believed. One of the internal guards came running up to us , "mam, mam it's so good to see you back we have missed you!" "Your baby boy is so beautiful and a precious gift." What a lovely welcome we had. I made my way to the learning centre taking each step looking all around me , nothing had changed just the tightened security the odd repaint job here and there . If I was honest with myself I did feel anxious still but it's amazing what you can push yourself to do subconsciously knowing it is a step towards self-healing. I came to the door of the learning centre and stepped inside. Jo was at her desk and got up from her chair to greet me.

"Dawn it is so good to see you!" We hugged each other for a few minutes It was so emotional that we had been brought together again. "Dawn thank you for coming today let me look at Jacob oh how handsome he is". The girls are all excited to see you both.

Jacob and I went upstairs to see the other teachers it was so good to see them again. Jo came and collected us from upstairs and told me that John the Head of security would like to show me around the compound to show me the new procedures that had to be followed.

John explained that all the windows were now fitted with metal shutters and were bullet proof and incase of any possible future attacks as soon as the alert was raised the shutters would come down automatically. I was shown outside and told incase of an emergency I would be taken underground . This I can't explain due to security reasons. If

When I returned to work Jacob and I were not together I could make my way to him underground where we would meet up. I felt reassured that John and Jo had gone to these lengths for Jacob and I. Jo knew I would have anxieties about this so had preorganised the briefing. I said my goodbyes and called David to pick us up outside.

I returned to work a week later, It felt good to be back with the familiar faces around me. Swimming classes started up again and the children were all excited to learn to swim. The building where the pool was had taken the brunt of the attack and you could see evidence of something that had gone on here. I looked up and noticed that there was a bullet-hole in the wall that had been missed , all the others had been filled in. It was still hard to believe what had happened here.

David and I had decided to hold Jacobs 1st birthday party here. Jacob would still have one back on Las Dunas but the staff and children were so kind to him it would be nice to have some fond memories from school. Jacob's cake was ordered from the fine Oasis bakery. Layer upon Layer of fruit. At the end of the morning session we all headed over the the crèche. The nannies had put a large board behind the table with Happy 1st Birthday Jacob and blue balloons with trains and a large picture of him. David had been cleared to come onto the compound and he joined us at the table. It was such a lovely birthday party , watching the young ones eating their jelly and luxurious mini cakes . Everyone enjoyed this little celebration. We all felt it wasn't only a celebration of Jacobs birthday but a celebration of moving forward, feeling stronger and positive in our lives.

Jacob was 11 months old when he experienced his first desert convoy adventure! A few of us had arranged to meet up by the front gates in our 4x4's. We packed our cooler box with Jacobs bottles, cucumbers and various nibbles. Not to forget the sun creams, and the essential gallons of water. You could dehydrate really quickly out in the desert within a few hours. Alison and Mark who had invited us along were experienced desert trekkers so we felt fairly safe. Steve the security guard also offered to come along. Mark had the correct instruments for the convoy. You had to be very well prepared and organized. We had Gprs , Maps, and Walkie Talkies etc...

Mark did a final headcount and we were on our way, we were off!. There were 6 or 7 vehicles behind us, we were really excited as we hadn't done anything like this before and it was a challenge. Especially with an eleven month old baby. The roads in front of us and behind were a mass of dust, and it was hard to visualize onto the road. But it was all part of the excitement, we headed off road. There was a certain technique driving on the sand, you couldn't drive straight ahead onto the sand you had to drive sideways on the crust of the sand. I looked back into the car and Jacob was giggling uncontrollably at the same time a little frightened. It was the bumpy ride which was amusing him and he didn't know what to make of it all. David and I started giggling with him His cheeks were shaking! About every twenty minutes we would have to stop to help each other out of the sand. Once your tyres had dug deep in to the sand there was no way of getting your car out unless you had a friend with a tow rope at hand. The men would tie the rope to the back of their 4x4's and would slowly but surely pull you out then move on again until the next vehicle got stuck.

There was something very beautiful about the desert, the miles and miles of dunes baking in the sun.
After about an hour's driving we stopped to eat our well packed lunches. We all gathered our large blankets and lay them down onto the sand. We shared our picnics with each

other.   Fresh   refreshing   melons   and sandwiches . Some had brought portable barbecues, I was a little nervous to be honest looking around for any insects Scorpions, the much talked about Camel spiders these spiders were known to grow very large luckily I only ever saw a baby one , so I was very careful where I was sitting! These insects were all well-known and witnessed creatures of the desert. After about a 30 minute break Our water supply was running down pretty thin , so a few of us decided to head back home the desert was a very different place in the evenings and once dark it would prove very hard to find the way back home again. A few of the convoy decide to stay behind and experience a night sleeping under the stars. Steve the security guard turned to us and said how fantastic that we had brought Jacob along and asked us how he was enjoying his little adventure. Steve said that he had done some amazing things in his lifetime, but the little man doing this at eleven months old is incredible. We wished everyone the best and headed our way home, luckily not getting stuck in the sand. David had finally cracked the sand dune driving . It took us around two more hours before we were home again. What a wonderful and unforgettable experience enjoyed by all. Once back at the villa I awoke , He needed a well-earned shower. We were all full of sand and would benefit a nice cool shower. We all slept very well that night.

Chapter 10

Our days in Saudi Arabia were filled with happy and fond memories of our friends, the bonding, the experiences, the crazy shopping trips to the souks! The many barbecues and parties. Once a year a May ball would be held where you would have the opportunity to dress up in your finest attire. The men would wear their very smart dinner jackets and dicky bows, and the women would wear their most glamorous dresses on. The evening would be followed with a disco and a lovely three course meal, and drinks of your choice. The community also made an effort to bring people together and this event always had a large turnout.

When family is not nearby you tend to create a circle of friends who you can grow to trust dearly, who you can rely on, these friends become your Saudi family and more than definitely become your friends for life. You need great shoulders to lean on when you miss your loved ones back home. We had decided it was our time to try something new, particularly for David as he wanted a new challenge and felt he couldn't move forward in his employment here. Leaving these friends behind would be far harder than you could possibly know. Our family unit had decided it was for the best, new beginnings lay ahead. New adventures , we all know when we make choices in our lives that they feel like the right ones to do. It was our time to leave, the right choice for our family …. It was Our time to say goodbye………..

Since leaving Saudi we have been through many changes in our life . We have lived in many countries and enjoyed our new adventures and meeting new friends.

Our first adventure was relocating to Northern Italy, a little town called Meina, where the streets were quaint and the scenic views were amazing, we lived on a hill in a little blue painted house. It had a large window overlooking the Lake Maggiore. It was so beautiful waking up to the beautiful views of the mist over the lake every morning. Jacob had settled into the local school. It was a sweet school all the children had to wear blue pinstriped blouse type overshirts , they had their own little bed separate from the classroom where they could take a little nap if they became sleepy. Our weekends would be spent walking around the many colourful markets and walking besides Italy's many glorious lakes.

David had decided after a few months that his new employment wasn't suitable for him, but he was glad of the experience. I was sad to go but appreciated that my husband had to be happy in his employment.

Next our Journey would take us to one of our favourite places we have had the privilege to live in, a little town called Ejica in the Andalusia region of Spain. We had many many lovely friends . The Spanish friends we made would often ate outside Al Fresco and enjoyed the warm weather while they could. Jacob enjoyed going to school here in this quaint little town he picked up the spanish language really quickly. We walked everyday through the streets of Ejica with our friends. Lola my spanish friend helped me adapt to the language continuously talking Spanish to me everyday. Our children were really good friends, it was such a comfort to have them. David and I were introduced to the headmaster and his wife on our initial arrival to the school, Santiago and Guana , their daughters Maria and Laura became great and wonderful friends of ours such a caring family, they would babysit for us a few times and always tell us how much they had enjoyed Jacob and discussed with us what he had learnt in Spanish and that he was starting to understand the language a bit better.

At the school where Jacob attended on special occasions the children would queue up for their portion of olive oil and bread in the school yard, they were so happy to receive it. Water hoses were used to douse the children in the playground on hot summer days in their swimming costumes the sounds of laughter could be heard through the streets. One of our fondest memories was when Jacob took part in the school concert and had to dress up as a bumble bee he had black tights, gold wings and a gold and black striped top, he looked so adorable, all the children took part in a short dance the crowds cheered at the children it was a wonderful evening.

We loved the European lifestyle it was so laid back , In the evening we would go down to the town square, here all the families would gather for Tapas and the children would happily play in the centre of the Square . It was a happy place to be. In Ecija there is a museum which holds one of the largest findings from an archaeologist site. Some pieces were nearly intact like the life-size figure of a roman man. Just a slight piece was missing out of one of his fingers. The find was discovered when they were building an underground car park. Obviously they had to stop after excavating, it took them finally ten more years to unearth all the treasures and the square was handed back to the local people to their delight. In the summer it would get very hot and unbearable. "Ecija" was known as the "Frying Pan" Of Andalusia. The streets would pull out there shades from the windows above and the avenues would be a comfort and cooler in the shade to enjoy a cool refreshing drink . We left Spain reluctantly as David's contract with the company he worked for came to an end. We stayed a few years in the United Kingdom and decided we would be financially be better off if we went back to Saudi Arabia as David's industry would always take us abroad and the salary was always that much higher. The land of sand was to become our home once again. By now Jacob had several drawbacks with his speech, we were to blame after moving to all these different countries and the changes in language. After being back in Saudi for a year or so David was headhunted for the job that would bring us to where we are now, but little did we know what our future had planned for us already.

And finally I can verify that dreams do come true prayers can be answered and life can change for the better. Never give up on hope, always follow your gut instinct that something is right. Don't judge yourself others will do that. Hold your head up high every single day and tell yourself you can do it. Take chances in life as they may not always come around again. And lastly, live life to the fullest always be thankful for the family and friends you have around you, because tomorrow you may not have them.

So here we are in the most beautiful place in the world. Switzerland in the canton of Nidwalden. Why me? Why us? I ask everyday. So so fortunate to be here, so grateful with all the love in the world surrounding us we couldn't be happier. We spend most weekends walking in the Alps and follow the many beautiful trails. One of our fondest memories is Snowshoeing on valentines night with a moonlit sky, so beautiful then finishing at a quaint little log cabin where we had a valentines meal it was so romantic.

Jacob has settled in well at his new school in Ennetburgen, making new friends, he has even Tobogganed down the Klewenalp on his own and taken part in many town festivals. Jacob is also tackling the language very well.

Jacob was assessed in Lucerne, Switzerland by an Austrian psychologist for Autism and Aspergers, but everytime the psychologists would come back with the same results, the little boy had tuned out and had convinced himself he would be moving on somewhere else soon. The psychologist told us for Jacob to settle down and move on we had to tell him we would be staying .

We have moved on now since May 29th, 2004. By writing this book and telling my story it will give me closure , the story had to be told.
I do suffer some days with flashbacks and anxiety attacks of Jacob and I and of our ordeal, but time has a way of healing .
Life is so kind to us right now and we are thankful for every special day we have . I spend most days with my lovely friend Paola who after all these years ended up in the same little village in Ennetburgen, who would of thought after all these years we would be brought together again to be friends here in

this beautiful country. Some friends are meant to be.

It's been a struggle, … but…. Jacob is here by my side alive and well and the most adorable supportive little boy you could ever wish to meet and love , I am grateful for every day I have.

One day I will tell Jacob the story when he is old enough to know how a little boy helped his mum to make it through one of the hardest days of her life and survive.

Sadly and unbelievably just before finishing this book ten years since the attack, David my beloved Husband , and father suddenly passed away, he had a massive heart attack and died in my arms. An undescribable pain is left in our hearts to carry forever. The same day that David died the remaining five terrorists responsible for the Al Khobar attacks were sentenced to death. David was so happy that justice had been done, how bittersweet he would die the same day..... A year to the day we arrived in Switzerland he was only 50 years old and such a happy and wonderful man. No words can describe how we all feel right now. One thing I am sure off is that I was loved like I feel I could never be loved again. We had so many plans and dreams to achieve so much more love to share together. One of our dreams was to finish writing my story. David would of wanted me to complete it. So here I am completing the end of my book without you by my side David.

I read the last few words we had written together out at his memorial service he was with me all the way writing my book and advising me , he was my rock my soulmate, so I only thought it right he should hear them. Jacob can't really understand why his daddy left he is now 10 years old and has a lot of memories to treasure but he has the same beautiful smile his father had and smiles every day for us. This makes me live on and gain my strength everyday I will survive .

I am so proud of Aimee and Ben for being by my side and for being there for me in my darkest moments. Their strength is amazing their father would have been so proud of them too. We as a family have so many wonderful memories. David and I had celebrated our 26th wedding Anniversary in October 28th 2014, just a few weeks before he died. We had a wonderful few days in the beautiful surroundings of Lake Bellagio, Italy, we took a boat trip across the lake to Lake Como and sat next to the lake and ordered and enjoyed a very sneaky early morning Aperol ,one of our favourite drinks, an orange spritzer with a slice of orange soda water and prosecco wonderful. We were to have several more that day too. I am oh so thankful for those beautiful memories and have to thank our wonderful friends Kay and Steve, for making it possible by taking care of Jacob for us. We all feel privileged to have had David in our lives even if it was only for a short while.

So our new Chapter and journey begins, all of us trying to rebuild our lives the best way we can. Sometimes in life you don't have the choice to do what you really want to do, you just try your best to move forward and to make the best of your life any way you can. We may look as though we are strong but underneath we hide our pain only ourselves know of.
Loosing David was and still is so painful to myself, and to our children. I believe he is watching over us and urging me on to finish this book. David would have been so proud that I would still be able to finish it .

Jacob and I have regretfully left Switzerland now with the amazing help of our dear family and friends Robin, Paola and David. I would like also to thank Adele and Jason our dear friends who stand by our side everyday and check to see how we are all doing .

Jacob has settled into his new school ,he is one brave little boy, he is so happy. I think he is channelling his energy, love and strength into being academically brilliant we are all so very proud of him too. He is a chip off the old block like his father was.

I have told Jacob that we will be staying here in Britain near our family as he needs security, love and stability in his life. We can find all this near our friends and family .

Ben and Aimee feel the loss the pain of their father too but continue to support us whatever way they can. Ben is also focused on starting his own business and has lots of super ideas and projects that I can't wait to see developed. Aimee lives in Cyprus for the meantime , she has several jobs that keep her on her toes, she will be home with her beautiful family in a year or two which will be lovely to have all my children so near to me again. We continue to support each other as the loving supportive family we always were and still are.

Life can be very cruel sometimes and you try to keep your head above water . I wish it had turned out differently and I had the opportunity to have had so many more years together with David and to grow old and to share more love and time with him , but sadly it cannot be.

You can choose to sink or swim in this world. Well as a family we choose to swim, to keep our heads high above the water to show David we will be strong and to live our lives as happy as we all can the lake may seem wide right now but I am sure one day and with the determination we will reach the shore, he would of wanted us to.

It was hard leaving Switzerland where we shared so many good memories and friends, we will return one day. Three months before David died we celebrated in Switzerland for his 50th Birthday with friends and family. David had a very special surprise gift, a flight in a glider flying above the Alps. David had a passion for aircraft and worked all his life in this industry. I am so glad he had the opportunity and the courage to do it. We will never forget how happy he looked the day he took off into the blue skies, we waved you off goodbye, you couldn't stop smiling at us, this is how I will remember you David.

Always ....

And Finally,

David I promise to look after all our children to hold my head up high not to look down at my feet, but look towards the stars for there you are my darling. You have all the answers to the universe now. I know I will see you again one day, So until them my sweetheart keep flying high, I carry your heart x

36338417R00123

Printed in Poland
by Amazon Fulfillment
Poland Sp. z o.o., Wrocław